Never Alone

Journeying Through Grief

By

Libby Teston Auers

Never Alone

Journeying Through Grief

First Publication

Published in the United States of America

Published by ATC Publishing LLC

P.O. Box 127

Senoia, GA 30276

ISBN: 978-1-7362222-4-9

DEDICATION

In loving memory of Loren and for our family who are a reminder that through God all things are possible and that I am NEVER ALONE.

TABLE OF CONTENTS

INTRODUCTION

"Have I not commanded you? Be strong and of good courage;
Do not be afraid, nor be dismayed, for the Lord your God is
with you wherever you go"
Joshua 1:9

What can one say to themself when they experience the death of someone they love that will bring peace and comfort back to their shattered life? Yes, for an exceptionally long time, your life does feel shattered.

In the years since my husband Loren's death, I have learned that the things we choose to do and the things we choose to say to ourselves are vastly different for each of us, and that it takes extremely hard and emotional work to begin to put the pieces of your life back together again. You may not choose to do the work that will eventually bring you to that peace and comfort for a very long time. Sometimes it can take years for someone to decide they are ready to do the work to make them feel alive once again. There have been many people that I have spoken to in these years since Loren's death that have stood in front of me, mouth wide open, as I share how I have come to a certain peace through this experience.

The "experts" will tell us that "death is death." That is truth. The "experts" will tell us there is "no ranking" death. That is truth. I have had the opportunity to speak with several people whose spouses have died, and I have spoken to others who have experienced the death of a loved one, be it a child, a parent, a sibling or a friend, and they have shared that how they experienced that grief was very different given the relationship.

My own mother and I have shared conversations on this subject. You see, my mother and father experienced the death of an infant at four months of age. My mother has experienced the death of both of her parents and ten months before my own husband died my mother experienced the death of her husband, six months short of their 60th wedding anniversary, my father. Our conversations were very poignant, and she has shared with me that each of these deaths brought a unique way of how she experienced grief.

I will also share that the way I have experienced the death of my father is very different than how I have experienced the death of my husband and how I have mourned each of them. Could it be because my father died amid Loren's illness? Could it be that ten months after my father's death my husband died, and I was thrown into the pain of losing my spouse and that that grief will be a forever journey with its own twists and turns? I suppose I will never know the answer to that question. I can only share what I know, and that is that the death of my father and the death of my husband have been two very different experiences in emotion and grief.

I do not pretend to be an "expert" on grief. In fact, I have said many times to those I have had conversations with on the subject, that I am only an "expert" on my OWN grief. I do feel that how we experience that grief, or more to the point, how we choose to LIVE with the grief after the death of someone we love IS a choice. How we look at the experience of our loved one's death and the pain that no doubt colors each day can affect the rest of our days here...positively or negatively.

So, this is what has brought me comfort and peace all these days since my husband left his physical body and returned HOME...

I believe I am NEVER ALONE. Yes, there have been many days I have been lonely. The world continues to go on. Our circle of people that surrounded us is no longer here. Why? I am certain there are many reasons. I believe the world does not want to see the pain of grief. Someone they knew, in the prime of their life, someone who was vibrant, healthy, handsome or beautiful and strong has died. That person they knew is no longer there by the side of the person that they knew as "one" with the other. The reality of what has happened in someone else's life is something none of us really wants to face. That is the explanation I have given myself in this life since Loren's death. I'm certain the reasons we find ourselves lonely could make up an entire chapter in a book.

My faith tells me that each moment of my day I am surrounded by God's loving protection. My heart tells me that Loren's love for me since his death has become far stronger, far more beautiful and far purer than while he was here in this life, and that his love surrounds me as well. These two things are what I tell myself at the start of each new day. These two things are what have brought me the most comfort and peace each moment of my day since Loren's death.

I have also found that when allowed to share our pain and grief about the death of a loved one that healing can begin, and with that sharing it becomes possible to encourage one another to look at life in a new way. There can be joy. There can be happiness. There can be peace. Because in truth we are ... NEVER ALONE ...

I begin "NEVER ALONE" where I ended "There Is No Randomness About Your Life" because in these years since Loren's death I still believe that the experience of his illness and death continues to have purpose. Every person that has come into my life, every experience I have had, whether painful or joyous, has served a purpose. When I sit with that knowledge, I am also aware that some experiences defy explanation. They defy my ability to discern "the purpose." So, I will wait until the time that I stand face to face with our Father for the understanding. It is then that HE will make it all perfectly clear.

What follows is the journey of a million miles … the beginning of a lifelong journey through grief …

~

May

2015

~

"Trust in the Lord with all your heart,
And lean not on your own understanding"
Proverbs 3:5

The devotional I read today does a much better job of explaining what I have been feeling at this time in my life. The line simply read, "There is no randomness about your life." I do not understand why we experienced the journey of Loren's illness or the journey that I am experiencing right now in my life ..."Lean not on your own understanding.", but it is most obvious to me that I am on "a path of HIS choosing." I am trying my best to remember that HE walks with me in this present journey, and I am trying my best to stay in the present by not fearing the future ... HE is already there. I am doing my best to allow HIS Spirit to direct my footsteps. I am allowing myself to grieve when those moments hit me, but I am doing my best to choose to find the joy in each day. HE wants me to and so does Loren. As Loren said just weeks before he passed, "I was always happy". Yes, he was, he chose to be. So will I.

*****

Today a special lady who knows my heart and has listened to me pour out my "soul" over this past year asked me to join her at a large craft fair in Gay, Georgia. I thanked her then and I thank her now.

It was a first time for me and something Loren and I had said we would do every year and never did.

I found this beautiful plaque and I had to bring it home. Maybe it is a way for me to explain what it is some are having trouble understanding about grief ... my grief. "It is well with my soul".

Only I know how I have grieved throughout this entire year. Deep grief of what we no longer had as husband and wife, and yes, possibly knowing deep in my soul what was to come even though I always tried to love, support and HOPE along with Loren. Now, although the tears do come (as my friend can attest to) "It is well with my soul" because I know that Loren's soul is at rest, is at peace and he is whole again.

It was his faith; it was our faith that allowed us to know that God was with us along the journey wherever it would lead. "It is well with my soul."

And I remember that I am NEVER ALONE.

It Is
Well
With
My
Soul

*****

For the first time in the three weeks since Loren's death I sat down at my desk at work and thought, "I have to call Loren to say hello and to tell him about"... That was our routine nearly every day at lunch time, even before he was sick. In that moment, the reality of Loren no longer physically by my side has crashed down upon me. It is always there, but there are moments that I experience that make that reality so much more painful. Like this one. The tears flow.

*****

Yesterday was three weeks since Loren died.

In the past couple of days I have had two people say to me, "I was talking to someone (the "someone" is never named) and they are 'worried' about you." I'm never told "why" they are worried about me, which I find interesting.

I imagine "they" are worried about me because I am not "grieving" in the manner that others think I should be grieving.

To all those well-meaning people I say this, apparently you were not among those walking as closely in the journey in the past year as some of the others in our lives were. If you had been you would know the many times that I cried as Loren and I experienced the many deaths of our life together along the way.

You would know how our life as we knew it was gone long before Loren's physical death, and how we mourned all of that for the past year. "Quality of life" was a term we had heard over and over again from the first day of Loren's diagnosis. We had NO "quality of life". We mourned that every day.

There have been those who have allowed me through the entire journey to sit with them and who listened to my pain and allowed me to cry healing tears. Yes, my husband is physically gone, but I have grieved his loss in MANY ways all through this past year. I have cried tears of sorrow, tears of fear and tears of exhaustion all throughout this time. If you were or ARE concerned, why didn't you see that?

I find it interesting that there are people that are "concerned about me" and yet in the past three weeks my phone has barely rung. I guess people have a much different way of showing concern. Their way of being "concerned" is to apparently speak to others about my grieving process.

To those people I say, while my phone is not ringing or you are not spending time with me so that I can share my grief with you on a more personal level, I am sitting at home alone at night, and go to bed at night with eyes swollen with tears and a heart broken with the pain of having lost my beloved of nearly 35 years. But you wouldn't know that, because during the day I choose to live. I choose to be "okay" because I promised Loren over and over again in this past year that I would be ... and that is what I intend to do.

If you haven't experienced this kind of grief than I will share with you that "Grief is different for everyone" and how they choose to share that with the world is as different as we are human beings.

And yes, the anger of grief is rearing its ugly head.

*****

"HE heals the brokenhearted and binds up their wounds"
Psalm 147:3

One month ago today. There are days I cannot believe that he is no longer here with me. The pain that I feel both physically and emotionally at times can be too much to take. I now know how it is very possible for one to die of a "broken heart." The pain is real. It is a pain that is felt so deep in the cavern of your chest that at times you cannot breathe. You gasp for air throughout your day, and you wake up (when you can sleep) in the darkness of your room and feel as if the darkness is enveloping you and dragging you down into a dark hole from which you will never find your way out.

****

"He who says he abides in HIM ought himself also to walk just as HE walked"

1 John 2:6

How beautiful it was to wake up to this tribute for Loren written by our son-in-law Michael.

"This is borderline rambling, but I promise it has a point."

"Today I had the privilege of hearing a retired Air Force Colonel speak about his experiences in Vietnam flying the F-4 Phantom. As a member of the 555th Tactical Fighter Squadron (the "Triple Nickel"), he was the first Weapons System Officer to earn flying ace status with six confirmed MiG kills. He didn't focus on himself much – he gave credit to the pilot, the weapons techs, and his crew chief and maintenance team, many of whom he remembered by name even after all these years.

Afterwards, I showed him this picture to see if he had flown on tail 762 (as seen on the nose gear). He did not fly on 762, but since the number is outlined in green, he said it belonged to the Triple Nickel. I did a little research and found that tail 64-0762 was, in fact, stationed at Da Nang Air Base but was destroyed by a mortar attack in 1967. Turns out the F-4 in the picture is 65-0762, a Block 28 Phantom that was transferred to the Republic of Korea Air Force in 1972. Loren served from 1975-1980 (in several locations including Korea) as a crew chief on F-105s, F-111s, and F-4s before his career at Delta Air Lines began.

Today also marks one month since Loren's passing. At his memorial service many of his co-workers from Delta Air Lines attended and had nothing but great things to say about his calm demeanor, relentless work ethic, and abilities as an engine mechanic and inspector. Just like the colonel who remembers the name of his Crew Chief, I know there will be many people who will remember Loren's name and the significant impact he had on their lives."

*****

Today I began something I really didn't want to. I began looking through some of Loren's things.

While going through Loren's nightstand I am reminded of the man he was and WHO he lived for each and every day of his life. There were so many books about our faith. Prayer cards, notes and things he would print off of the internet that evidently would strike a chord in his heart and soul.

Many things would bring tears to my eyes as I read each of them wondering what he could be thinking about at that time to be touched in such a way to keep what he had come across. Then I came across this. The only thing handwritten, and of course I reached for our bible.

I first wondered when he had written it as there is no date. Then I read the scripture. So Loren. There was NOTHING material on this earth that meant anything to him, nothing. All that mattered to him was his family. I am left wondering if this is a message from him, letting me know of the "treasure" he has found and what awaits me, what awaits all of us, if we will but surrender ourselves to HIM. What a gift it was to find this as I was dreading this next part of the journey...

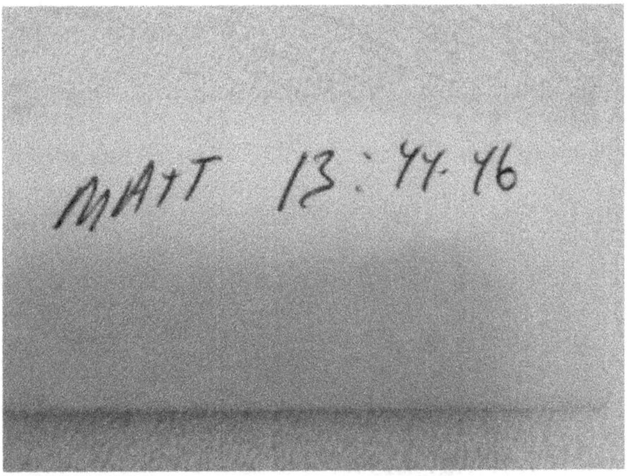

Matthew 13: 44-46

44 "Again the kingdom of heaven is like treasure hidden in a
field, which a man found and hid; and for joy over it he goes
and sells all that he has and buys that field.
45 Again, the kingdom of heaven is like a merchant seeking
beautiful pearls, 46 who, when he had found one pearl of great
price, went and sold all that he had and bought it.

*****

It has been a while since I've been able to write. It's been a while since I have been able to pray ... really pray. Everyone assures me that this is "normal". That it is part of the "grief process". Whatever that is. I am definitely aware that I have reached another "stage" of grief.

For those of you who have been here to listen, who have allowed me to share my grief with you, you know that after Loren died I would say, "where is he"? and "where have the past 34 years gone because I can't see him, I can't feel him. It's almost as if he never existed." I've been waiting for that time to come when all I would do is "see" him. It has, but with that has come the anger and at times the overwhelming pain and lonliness.

I guess I feel "normal" now. I see him everywhere I go now. Sitting in the lot of the gas station ... he walks away from the car towards the cashier with his long lean body always with that proud military walk and stance that he had. Even my trip through the drive through of McDonald's after church this morning. As I sat waiting I was seeing him, as I used to many Sunday mornings, waiting and watching while he went in to place an order. As I sit and fold laundry I see him in my minds eye sitting on the floor folding laundry. Always very precisely folded, again the military man in him. Everywhere, everywhere now I am reminded of him. Where has he gone? Why did it take so long for me to "see" him?

Maybe because this week little by little I have started to go through some of his things or maybe it's just the passage of time. Several people told me that I was numb. I didn't think I was. After all how could you possibly be numb with everything that we had been through? I keep pushing myself through the difficult days knowing it is all "part of the process", but this anger part I don't want. It's not pretty and it makes you want to shut yourself off from the world, although the world is doing a pretty good job of that without my help at all. Maybe it's the loneliness that is making me angry. I'm not sure. I find that I am a study in contradiction at this time. I don't want to be alone, but I do at the same time. I guess it just depends on the who (which there haven't been many who's around) but also the when. I have been told by a few people that "it's so difficult for people to know what to do or say", yes, I imagine it is, but it's better than not saying anything at all ... unless it's "I already know how I am going to grieve if she goes before me." Yes, I was actually told this today. I couldn't quite believe it myself and good luck, I sure hope it works as you have planned. Good God in Heaven! I could barely believe what I was hearing. Enough of that ...

I guess my point is that there most certainly are different stages of grief. I find myself wondering, "Is this where I am supposed to be right now? Is it too soon for this part of my grief, or is it too late?" I don't know, but I am doing my best to find my way through it and I have become very much aware that there are few people who want to help you through it. Maybe no one is supposed to, maybe you are supposed to do it on your own. Again, not something I think anyone really knows "how to do". But while I'm trying to figure it all out my mantra will be "Lord give me your peace at all times and in every way" because I think that is the only way one may be able to "get through it".

*****

This morning I saw a photo of our Blessed Mother on the internet and I was taken back to Easter Vigil. Loren was in hospice and we were able to go to the chapel for Easter Vigil Mass.

His bed had been placed near the statue of the Virgin Mary to the side of the chapel. He had become agitated after the move down the hallway. I looked up and said, "Honey look, it's our Mother Mary. She is looking down on you and praying for you. Let's pray to her." I started whispering the "Hail Mary" next to his ear and he started praying with me. He immediately began to calm, and we whispered it over and over again until Mass began. Loren was devoted to our Blessed Mother. His rosary was always with him. Whether it was his dress pants, his work pants, in the console in his car it was with him, his entire life. Throughout his illness his rosary was always nearby him in the hospital. Praying to Our Mother gave him a peace that was beyond comprehension.

I am certain that SHE was there alongside her SON and THE FATHER to welcome Loren "HOME". This photo brings me joy this morning.

~

June 2015

~

"Now may the God of hope fill you with all joy and peace in believing, that you may abound in hope

by the power of the Holy Spirit."

Romans 15:13

*****

Tonight I enjoyed dinner with friends. It was so nice to sit with friends who knew the two of us for years and who walked beside us through this difficult past year. One of them shared a conversation with me that he had recently with one of Loren's co-workers from Delta Air Lines. During the conversation they spoke about Loren and the co-worker told him that things "just are not the same" without Loren there. My heart needed to hear those words. I needed to know that Loren has not been forgotten, as he thought he would be. I needed to know that time, as short as it has been since his death, has not removed Loren from their minds.

*****

I am trying so hard to remember that every day my feet hit the floor is the "first day of the rest of my life" ... and a day that means the possibility of many "firsts". But it is also another day to miss him more than yesterday ... today is one of those days ... finding it a challenge to remember that I am NEVER ALONE.

*****

The end of the school year has come and I have traveled to northeast Ohio to spend much needed time with my Mom. We have not seen each other since Loren's death in April. Our lives are running parallel to each other's. We are both learning to live with the death of our husbands. I am glad to be here.

*****

It has been three weeks and it is time to return home...I have made many decisions about my life since being away. Decisions I never thought I would be making on my own, and certainly not at this time in my life. I will admit I am afraid ... but I must keep remembering ...

I am NEVER ALONE.

~

July 2015

~

"Behold, God is my salvation, I will trust and not be afraid; For YAH, the Lord, is my
strength and song; HE also has become my salvation."
Isaiah 12:2

*****

Today I am being reminded that "There Is No Randomness About Your Life." A reminder that my life experiences are to be looked at as "treasures". No matter how difficult. "Radiant treasures" full of HIS love and glory for me ... for all of us. I will do my best to find comfort and peace in this.

*****

It is 5:30 in the morning and I am sitting here having done one of what will become many "firsts" I am certain, since Loren's death. I am headed back to the airport, and back home to Atlanta, after what was a last-minute decision to take a trip and without a doubt Loren had prompted me to do so.

Since returning from visiting with my family up north, other than breakfast with a dear friend and a visit for a few hours from my son and grand babies, I have sat alone in this house. Not that I have wanted to, but everyone's lives are going on and mine is sitting still. The weekend had been difficult emotionally, and I sat and watched hours of my jewelry obsession on a shopping network. This weekend there is a jewelry event up north in Pennsylvania featuring my favorite jewelry designer for the Fourth of July holiday and I was full of sadness because Loren and I would often attend these events together.

While I sat the other evening this voice, yes it was really a voice, resonated in my head. "Check the flights to Philly"... so I did. The flights were wide open on a holiday weekend? Really? Should I go? I sat there for hours going back and forth in my mind and each time I had decided I was not going there was that voice again saying "GO"!!!! So, I did. I put my big girl panties on, and I went. I had decided weeks ago I was not going to go because "It's just going to be too hard" ... Loren and I ALWAYS were together at these events. I had asked Marie, my daughter, if she would go with me but her work schedule would not permit. So, like many times lately, I had decided it would just be easier to say “no” than to deal with something on my own that would be too painful.

But I realized while sitting and contemplating whether I should go or not that my whole life is now going to be filled with "the first time without Loren."... MANY times. If I continue to postpone all of those "firsts" my life will become a series of not living life because of the pain. I would be sitting here feeling alone forever.

I'm happy I did it. I know Loren was smiling down with that huge, gorgeous smile of his that he was always known for.

Throughout the entire time away I felt his presence with me. Several times while sitting there a shiver would literally run through my body and I would just smile realizing he was right there beside me. He was listening to me laugh and he was watching as I received the hugs of so many people. It was good ... it will continue to be good ... and as I promised him so many times during the year that he was ill, "I'm going to be okay." A "first time" of so many more to come ... and I am NEVER ALONE.

*****

Every day is a challenge, and every day is a choice to be happy as you struggle to figure out exactly who you are now when a part of you is missing.

*****

Today I accomplished what I had set out to do. Today I felt as if I had "purpose" once again. Today I submitted my request to the publishing company to use the passages from their devotional for the journal I wrote during Loren's illness. Because I wanted to be sure I had everything in order to complete the request I ended up reading completely through everything I had written. It took most of the day, but I completed the paperwork and submitted it. Then Loren and I had a conversation. An extremely tearful one on my part, but I could feel him near, and I could feel his encouragement, just like he had always done all of our lives together. He always had far more confidence in me than I ever have had in myself. One of the many gifts that he has left here for me. The gift of his confidence in me.

The rest of the evening has been difficult. My mind has been full of the memories of that last day together three months ago. The hours of sitting next to him, holding his hands, stroking his arms and humming to him ... releasing him to our Heavenly Father. The memory of him opening his eyes, trying to speak, the tear rolling down his face, and taking his last breath with my arms wrapped around him. I'm not sure those memories will ever fade. Honestly, I am not sure I want them to, even though they overwhelm me with emotion when I cannot let them go.

I laid on the couch and I stayed there, transporting myself back to three months ago. With all the emotion of those final hours and minutes ... I just stayed there ... and I let the tears flow. It doesn't happen often. Most of the time I would say "I'm okay", but tonight I longed for Loren to be here telling me how proud he was of me for moving forward with something that means so much to the two of us. It is his story. It is our story. It is one that needs to be shared with others that are in pain, because I have come to the realization that no one wants to hear the pain of someone grieving. It is just far too painful for others to see and hear the mourning of someone else. But those of us who mourn need to know we are NEVER ALONE.

Hours later I climbed the stairs and fell into bed reaching for my devotional. When I opened it the quote I read spoke to me. It reminded me to go to HIM with my pain and my sorrow and to place my trust in HIM. I choose to go to HIM and affirm my trust in HIM. To believe in HIS unfailing love and that HE will lift me up continually and watch over me so that I can keep my promise to Loren ..."I'll be okay honey, I'll be okay"...

*****

I'm feeling unkind today. I have never thought of myself as an "unkind" person, but today I am feeling that way. Today I am giving myself permission to feel that way.

I sent a text to someone today because of something I plan to do on Monday. I have not heard from this person since Loren's funeral months ago, in fact, I have not heard from many people since Loren's funeral. Not a text, not a phone call...nothing. I do not understand it and it is painful. This person returned my text with an apology for not having reached out to me before now. I wasn't sure how to respond to that. Am I supposed to excuse it? Because it is painful that I have become non-existent for so many people. I know. I get it. Everyone's lives are moving on. So is mine. Without Loren. And apparently without a lot of the people that were in our life.

I have spoken to a few people about this recently and they tell me, "Oh, you know, it's hard for people. They don't know what to say"... honestly, I don't either. My husband died three months ago after a long illness and I don't know what to say to others that are going through the same thing. How is that? I'm not sure. What I will share with you is that "words" are not necessary. Your presence is. Your heart and your "listening" is. Hold someone's hands in yours and "listen." Don't attempt to "say something". Listen. And when their tears begin to flow allow it. ALLOW it. And when they need to curl up in a fetal position collapsing into your chest, ALLOW it. This is where the healing begins. Not in trying to find the "right words." There are none.

I know it is difficult to think about a man that you knew who was never sick and who took such good care of himself dying. But he did. He had brain cancer. He was very ill. And he died. But part of him goes on because part of him was me. And part of me was him since the time I was seventeen years old, and now I am alone. Physically alone. I believe Loren's presence and his love always surrounds me, but that is not quite the same as someone's physical presence. Someone who you woke up with, went to bed with and did everything in between those times every day for nearly thirty-five years. So, whether it is me, or someone else you might know who has a loved one who is very ill, and you are there for them now, be there for the one who is left behind afterward. Do not be afraid that you do not know what to say ... just reach out to them. Reach out to them even if it is nothing more than a text.

Today I am giving myself permission to feel the anger, the pain, the resentment and the unkind thoughts ... tomorrow I will relax and let it go ... with love ... I will be okay ... because I promised I would ... I am NEVER ALONE.

*****

It is Sunday morning, and I am out having breakfast ... alone ... again. Not that every day doesn't have its difficult times, but Sunday mornings can be even more so. On Sunday mornings we were up and out to church and we would either stop for breakfast, or Loren would make us breakfast when we came home. This morning I am struck by how I see an elderly couple walk in front of me and I am questioning "why"? Why weren't we given that gift of growing old together? Why was a man who stood so tall, who took such good care of himself, who was hardly sick a day in his life, why is he gone? I struggle each day still with trying not to question HIS reasons for bringing Loren HOME and for leaving me here in a world that does not understand the pain and loneliness of grief and my shame of looking at someone else and asking, “why us ... and not them”?

As time passes, I become more aware that this is going to be a lifelong journey. No, it is not "over" in a few months, nor will it be over in a year or even more. It will be a forever journey ... no matter where life takes you. And I do my best to remember ... I am NEVER ALONE.

*****

Another night of watching "mindless" TV. While sitting here my mind has wandered from one thought to the next of Loren, especially since the opening scene of the program I am watching was in Ireland. Enniskillen to be exact, which was our first stop after we landed in Dublin in 2009. I recently looked through the photo book that I had put together from that visit to Ireland. As I looked through it there was a sadness that came over me because we had talked so often in the year before he became ill about going back to Ireland for another vacation.

I also became aware of something rather odd ... or maybe it is not. Maybe a so called "expert" on grief would be able to shed some light on this. When Loren died I had made copies of some of my favorite photos of him and had purchased frames to put them in to display them in the family room, but I will not look at them. Why won't I look at them? Maybe it is because it will conjure up too much pain and subconsciously I realize it, so I just won't look at them. Strange isn't it? And as I realize this my mind has also wandered to that last twenty-four hours as I walked him HOME and remembering the last words I ever heard from his mouth. I knew in that moment that it would be the last time I would ever hear them from him ... he uttered "I love you"... Maybe that is why I cannot look at his pictures ... maybe I would expect to hear those words if I stared at his pictures long enough ... How blessed I am that those were the last words I ever heard him speak.

*****

Today I went to Delta Air Lines where Loren spent his entire adult life earning a living and providing for his family. My visit there was long overdue. I had wanted to do something for this Delta "family" that had done so much for us in this past year. Throughout his illness they continually let Loren know that he mattered. I will always be full of gratitude to them for that, and I wanted to let them know how much they mattered to Loren and to me. Several times while on the drive there I fought back tears and I did a fairly good job of it until I was standing there in that place where he had stood five days a week for nearly thirty-three years. There is a distinct smell to that workplace ... one I had smelled every day on Loren's uniforms when he would come home from work. After a time of standing there having conversations with Loren's Delta family the familiar smell began to overwhelm me and the tears came. Our senses have a way of holding so much emotional connection ... it most certainly did for me today. But sitting here this evening remembering the day I am happy that I went. It was good talking to the men that were connected to Loren in that place.

*****

Today is one of those days that I guess you could say I am feeling "paralyzed" with grief. Literally. When I woke up this morning that is about all I did. Wake up. I've laid here in this bed staring up at the ceiling for over an hour. My mind was telling me you must get up, you must get moving. You have lunch plans ... you don't know how many times I thought to myself, "no, no lunch plans today. I'm going to send a text and cancel"... I want to be alone in my self-pity today, I want to be alone in my thoughts of Loren, I want to be alone in my grief. And then God, because HE is "all that", HE has my friend send me a text ..."See you at 11:45!" HA! Well just snap me out of my funk God!

I sat up in the bed and I picked up my devotional. This day's reading talked about how HE knows my path is so very difficult and how my life is dull, VERY dull at this moment, and it talked about "SPARKLING" surprises! God knows how much I LOVE things that "sparkle", so why not my life? God always has surprises right around the bend.

I suppose it is time that I need to snap out of it and get myself together. I want to be ready for those surprises when they happen ... HE has a path laid out for me, I will try to be full of joy while I wait for HIM to reveal it to me ... one foot in front of the other today ... here I go ... I am NEVER ALONE.

"Blessed be the God and Father of our Lord Jesus Christ,
the Father of mercies and God of all comfort"
2 Corinthians 1:3

*****

It has been an interesting couple of weeks for me emotionally.

My daughter Marie and I have shared many conversations about how I have been feeling and has encouraged me to share them. She will tell me as we get ready to say goodbye that "you need to journal that on Facebook, right now! Do it!" That's my daughter. I have always told her she is far stronger, and far braver than her mother. And much like her father has always had far more confidence in me than I do myself.

The joy of spending time with Marie and Michael before another deployment was a special time and yet a time of sadness as well. Too often during this present time with them I was transported back to the time when news of their impending deployment came, and Loren was in the hospital receiving his chemo treatment. Dr. Dunbar, Loren's neuro-oncologist, moved heaven and earth to get his treatment completed in time for us to go to Oklahoma City to spend time with them before they left. My mind wanted to return to that time.

Saying goodbye to them this time was even more difficult. A difficult time that led to a deep feeling of loneliness and abandonment, not that those feelings are not with me often, but made worse at this time, and those feelings have consumed me for several days now since leaving them. But I have learned that I must allow myself to go there. I must allow myself to feel all those feelings rather than to stuff them down to continue my healing journey.

I had an interesting experience this week, which once again has shown me how far I have come in this journey known as grief. I had lunch with someone more than five years into her own grief journey with the loss of her husband. In all honesty I must say I walked away quite disturbed. I am not sitting in judgment of this woman. I have realized that we all heal at our own pace, and in our own time, and in our own way. I know that healing takes work. Very hard work each day, and frankly some are not ready to do the work. It was apparent to me during our conversations that we had made very different choices as to how we were going to live our lives, and I walked away knowing that four years from now that is not where I want to be. In fact, I am quite certain I was not there even in "the beginning". Oh yes, I have had times of deep sorrow. I'm not sure where the “knowing” I did not want to be "there" has come from. Perhaps it was that Loren continually told me "I just want you to be okay”, and I have realized that it is not just because I promised Loren that I would, but because I WANT to be. I want to “be okay”. But it is very hard work every day to do this by yourself. And I continually have to remind myself that I am really NEVER ALONE.

So here is the part Marie says I should share. Life is about loving and caring and showing kindness to one another. Or it's supposed to be, right? Then how come when there is someone that we know who is in pain, alone, feeling abandoned, how come we don't reach out? No phone calls, no texts, no notes? Is it too much to ask to care about one another in that way? If the answer is "yes" then there should be no question as to why the things that are happening in this world are happening. Because we are not even caring enough about our brothers and sisters right here in our own circle.

It is almost the dawn of a new day ... I pray that we all might remember to practice love and kindness for one another along the way. And remind each other that we are NEVER ALONE. How did I do Mimi?

*****

I love finding these little gifts ... it has been a couple of difficult, if not despairing hours as I decided to begin the sorrow filled journey of going through Loren's things, all the while "talking" to him and remembering so many special occasions. While going through one of his suits I found this. "Peace"... I believe he is asking me to find peace with my decision to do this today. How I love and miss him.

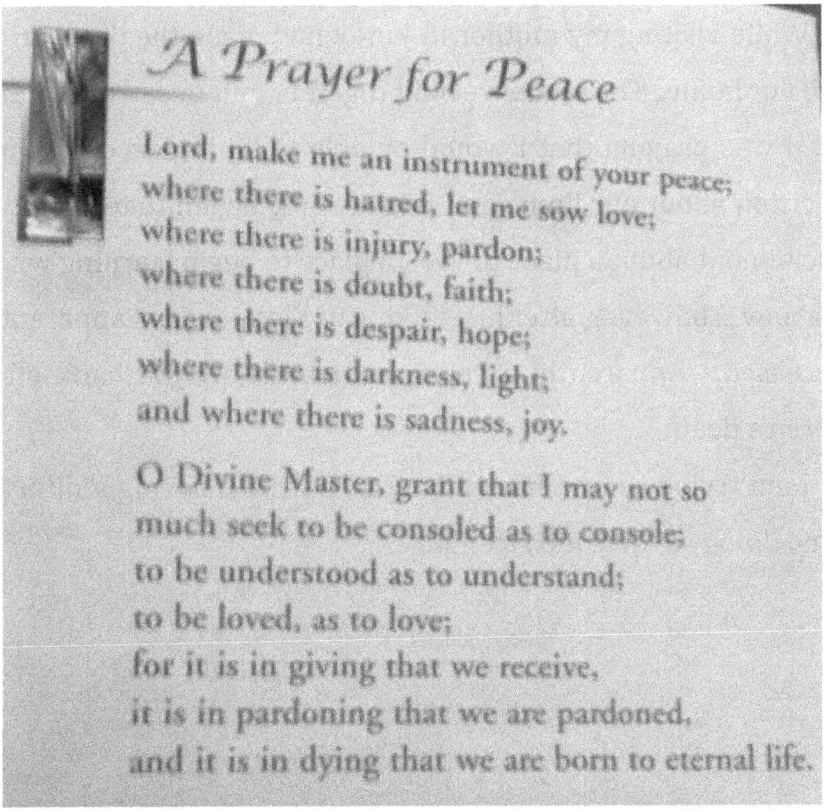

A Prayer for Peace

Lord, make me an instrument of your peace;
where there is hatred, let me sow love;
where there is injury, pardon;
where there is doubt, faith;
where there is despair, hope;
where there is darkness, light;
and where there is sadness, joy.

O Divine Master, grant that I may not so
much seek to be consoled as to console;
to be understood as to understand;
to be loved, as to love;
for it is in giving that we receive,
it is in pardoning that we are pardoned,
and it is in dying that we are born to eternal life.

*****

I have just watched the silver jeep pull out of the driveway ... yet one more thing I have "let go of" in the past few days. Loren enjoyed his old jeeps so much. It is just one more task of so many I have had to do ... but, I am thankful to Loren's friend who has continued to be here for me and help me however he can.

*****

While visiting my mother in June I had made the decision to sell our home. The home we built together and raised our family in. I was praying that I would be able to be at peace with my decision about our home and had actually begun to feel a bit of excitement about a place to "be", a place to begin learning who I am now ... however, after just talking to a lender, I am apparently deceased. Apparently a red tape debacle by the bank after Loren's death.

I am trying to find humor in that, but I am having a difficult time doing so. Give me strength ...

*****

"For every creature of God is good, and nothing is to be refused
if it is received with thanksgiving;
for it is sanctified by the word of God and prayer"
1 Timothy 4:4-5

It is 11PM ... I am curled up in bed and I have quiet music playing ... music that played throughout the year of Loren's illness during his hospital stays and a constant while in hospice ... exhale ...

*****

The phrase "the morning after"... could pertain to any number of things. In my personal experience it references Loren's death. And truth be told I could say from the moment of his diagnosis. I knew from that moment I was, no, WE were going to be "different." I had a conversation with someone the other day who shared with me about a friend of hers whose husband died in October. She told me that she and her husband were talking and her husband remarked about the "sadness" he could see in their friends eyes but that the sadness was also carried in her body, and he told her, "I don't think she will ever be the same." She looked at me waiting for my response. I hesitated a moment and said, "The truth is, she won't." I won't. No one who has experienced the death of someone they love will ever "be the same" again. And we can decide what it is we WILL be. We can remain broken and in the depths of sorrow. We can remain angry and bitter and allow our world to be colored by the pain. Or we can decide to put our feet on the floor each day and look for the beauty that is all around us. We can be still and spend time in the silence to FEEL our loved one's presence that surrounds us, and LIVE...THIS...LIFE. We can try our best to find the reason WHY we are still here. We can do our best to understand that our own purpose here is not complete. Go out there and find it!

*****

I have feared many things in this past year, but most of all was the fear of losing my husband. I have had so much loss in my life in this past year. Not just my husband. This past week has been a difficult time for me. Even when I stop now and allow myself to reflect on the entire year, from the diagnosis through the yearlong treatment without any remission for Loren, and the moment that we were told there was nothing left medically that could be done for him it seems so distant. Like there is a thick fog that is protecting my psyche, keeping even memories of Loren from getting too close. I have spoken to a few people about this. I have shared that I cannot seem to pull up memories of Loren and hold them close. It's as if this man that was a part of me for more than half my lifetime was only in my imagination. I have difficulty looking at his photos for some reason right now, but when I do it's as if I had conjured up his existence in my life in my mind.

Shortly after Loren died a friend sent me a copy of "A Grief Observed" by C.S. Lewis. I had never read it or seen the movie which is based on the book. It is a book written by Lewis about his wife who died. Last week while going through some things I found a card I had tucked away with a handwritten note from Loren. These little notes were few and far between from him. Not because of lack of “feeling” from him, but because he was a man of very few words. I am certain that is why it was so special to me and why I had kept it. The note is not dated which I find interesting, but the words he wrote were so perfect for what I am feeling right now. I have read it every morning and every night since finding it last week. I climbed into bed tonight read the card and his note to me and then picked up "A Grief Observed". My friend who sent me the book included a beautiful letter and told me that I would know when the time was right to read the book. I am not really certain there is a "right time" or not, but I have not even finished reading the forward by Madeleine L'Engle and I am struck by the fact that she and C.S. Lewis feel as I do about their memories of their loved ones. They describe the fear of the loss of their memory of the one they loved and lost. I almost feel as though I have amnesia. My memory has never really been that good anyway. Not like Loren's. God, he could remember EVERYTHING! Until the cancer took over, and then it was just his short-term memory that he had difficulty with. He could remember in unbelievable detail things from thirty or forty years ago! His best friend Mike told me that he enjoyed spending the nights at the hospital with him when he came to visit him. They shared so many memories ... memories Loren would recall that even HE had forgotten about until reminded by Loren.

"No photograph can truly recall the beloved's smile. Occasionally a glimpse of someone walking down the street, someone alive, moving, in action, will hit with a pang of genuine recollection. But our memories, precious though they are, still are like sieves, and the memories inevitably leak through. "This quote taken from the forward of "A Grief Observed" is EXACTLY how my head and my heart feel. I pray my fog begins to lift so that when I close my eyes and try to bring those memories to the forefront, they are not shadows but become crystal clear. I wonder if that is where a lot of the sadness comes from for those of us who grieve ... there is too much fog, and we cannot see our beloved with the clarity that we long for ...

A time to remember I am NEVER ALONE ...

~

August 2015

~

"The Lord will guide you continually, and satisfy your soul in drought, and strengthen your bones; You shall be like a watered garden, and like a spring of water, whose waters do not fail."

Isaiah 58:11

*****

As August began so did a new beginning. One without Loren physically by my side but relying on my belief that both he and God were guiding me every step of the way, and the need to stay strong and firm in that belief became a true exercise in faith and patience ... to remember I am NEVER ALONE.

*****

I am starting this day listening to Paul Cardell's version of "Redeemer" ... I needed to hear this beautiful piece of music today.

Today's devotional reading has reminded me to stay close to God, that he will guide me and guard me ... it reminds me to continue to rely on HIM because HE is right beside me.

I am relying on you Lord to guide my steps and help me to realize that YOU are already there around the next bend waiting for me ... be with me each moment of this day. Help me to know that I am NEVER ALONE.

*****

Today I am a mixed bag of emotions. Choose the emotion; I am probably feeling it. I also am aware that my heart is full of gratitude and thanks. Thankful to God who has carried me through the most difficult journey in mine and Loren's life and thankful to HIM who sustained us in every way possible through the love of HIS servant people. And thankful to my husband who gave of himself every day of his life to his family. His love of God and his love for his family defined who he was. Loren, whose only thought on the day of his diagnosis was "I just want you to be okay." Neither one of us knew what was ahead of us that day in April 2014, and sometimes I struggled with keeping my eyes on the Lord as HE directed our path. But not Loren. Loren never lost hope. He never lost faith. He never lost trust in our Lord. But being human, we did find that sometimes sorrow did fill our hearts. Sorrow of what had been. Sorrow of what may be. My life has continued to feel uncertain. I have struggled with fear. I have struggled with trust and the ability to stay prayerful. I have continued to rely on Loren to show me strength and trust in our Lord. I have struggled with so many emotions and not wanting to "let go" but knowing in my heart that the only way to go forward in this life is to "let go"... and to allow God to work in my heart and mind. It has been a difficult few weeks as I have tried to do that.

Having found this place which will become my new home, my new place "to be" in this world I struggle with this knowledge. This is the place where I will try to figure out who I am now. How is it that something that would normally cause such excitement and happiness is also filling me with such anxiety, fear and sadness? As I shared, I am experiencing every emotion possible. But today I am remembering to give thanks to our Father in Heaven and to Loren. I close my eyes and I imagine Loren having a conversation with our Father. "Lord I want her to be okay. Will you help me to watch over her? Will you help me to guide her footsteps and give her peace? I just want her to be okay." He is helping to take care of me now just like he did while he was here and my love for him in the nearly four months he has been gone has only deepened.

I thank my family and friends who have continued to be here for me. Those who listen to my sorrow and lift me up in prayer. I ask that you continue to pray for me. This will not be an easy time as I move forward along this path God has me on. And I must try to remember that I am NEVER ALONE.

*****

So often in the last four months I have felt overwhelmed. Many days upon waking in the morning I have not wanted to put my feet on the floor as that would mean that I would have to face the stark reality of being physically alone. Yes, I have friends and family around me, but since I was eighteen years old Loren was a part of my life and the man that I had chosen to share the rest of my life with. Thirty-four years; it wasn't enough. Most days I feel like a part of my insides has been permanently ripped out. The journey of the past 18 months has taken a toll on me, I look in the mirror and I often have no idea who is looking back at me.

Somehow I put one foot in front of the other and move throughout my days. I have come to realize that the "somehow" is only by God's grace. I know that I am not the only person in this world who has lost a spouse. That fact is not lost on me. But when this happens to you it certainly can feel like that most days. You feel so isolated, even in a room full of people. And you feel so very lonely.

It has been a trying couple of weeks, and I have been so emotional as I have discerned a huge decision in my life, and even after making the decision I have felt uncertain.

But today I have been able to spend several hours in this place I have decided is where I will "be". The inspection was being done by a friend of Loren's who he had worked with at Delta Air Lines and who has his own home inspection business. When I first arrived for the inspection, he shared something that set the tone for me the entire time I spent there this morning.

When I walked through the door, he was standing in the living space and when he saw me, he said, "Welcome home Libby"! I had a difficult time holding back my emotions in that moment. And then he said, "I think you have made a wonderful choice." They were the perfect words, words I so needed to hear, because in those words I felt both Loren and God saying to me, "We are walking with you and you are trusting in the journey." To Loren's friend I am sure it was just a kind greeting, but to me they were so much more.

Today, I feel God's grace picking me up and carrying me through this time in my life. One moment, one day at a time. It is very hard a lot of days to feel that right now, but I am trying ... and I am NEVER ALONE.

*****

The waves of grief keep crashing in on me each night lately as I lay down to sleep, and I find myself asking HIM "Why"? Why would HE take Loren away from me? I cry out in distress as if it is a punishment.

So often when we go through difficult times we may feel that we are being "punished". We might admonish ourselves for past transgressions or perhaps we might feel as if we have fought against God's will in our lives. I have found myself feeling that way often in the past year and a half and needed to feel God's loving forgiveness.

Right now, I need to find myself in a place once again where I feel in my heart and soul that what has happened in my life is not "punishment" but that it is my life's journey that God has put me on. And that Loren's death was his path. Lately that has not been the way I have been feeling as I deal with the monumental task of preparing to leave this home that Loren and I had shared for nearly thirty years together ... alone. But I am trying to take it one day at a time, one task at a time and not over think it. I am glad my realtor suggested what he did to me, which was to not put my home on the market until I had found a new place to purchase, or I am sure I'd be out of my mind right now.

I need to remember now more than ever that I am NEVER ALONE.

*****

Tomorrow I will do something I have never done before. At fifty-four years old, for the first time in my life, I will have a home ... alone. I have always been someone's daughter, someone's wife, someone's mother, in a place provided by someone else. I will still have a home provided by someone else. The man who loved me for all my life. The man whose only concern in the past year was that I was "going to be okay". I know he has been walking beside me in these last four months guiding my path along with our Heavenly Father, but even so I have felt so alone while I have begun the journey of moving forward. How is it that although as old as I am for the very first time in my life I feel like an adult?

As emotional as I have been these past couple of weeks I cannot even begin to imagine what tomorrow afternoon will feel like or what it will feel like when I walk out the door of the home that I shared with Loren for almost 30 years. I try not to think about it too often ... for now I will be like Alice In Wonderland as she comes to the fork in the road ... and the Cheshire cat says to her "it doesn't matter" which direction I take ... who am I kidding?

*****

Tomorrow is going to be an amazing day!

After work today I went by what will become my new home to visit with Bob who has been painting it and doing some other things on my list of things I wanted to have done before moving in. He is a special person, and I am so blessed that his daughter-in-law, another pretty special person, connected me with him.

Another person I am blessed to know is Jeff from work. We had a conversation a few weeks ago and I shared with him my concerns about needing to take care of some things with my house before it can be put on the market. This man has put together a small army and they will come tomorrow and tackle a number of things that have been sorely neglected since fall of 2013 when Loren started not feeling well. Tonight, while my mind raced back and forth between both "homes" and the "to do" list just keeps on growing it was hard to concentrate on the drive home.

As I pulled into the street I was compelled to look up ... do you see her? God's guardian angel right in front of me hovering over my house.

Blessings will abound tomorrow as more than twenty people have volunteered their Saturday to help someone they do not even know. I am overwhelmed by their kindness and willingness to serve. My thanks and gratitude in prayer for all of them tonight as I lay here remembering that I am NEVER ALONE. God bless, sleep well.

*****

"Miracles"... A mere "shift in perception." It has been nearly five months since Loren began his new life. Yes, I could have written he died. I could have written passed away. I could have written any number of things. I choose to say, "he went HOME" or "began his new life." A "shift in perception" or as some might say, "words have power." The words I choose to use most of the time exemplify my "shift in perception." That is my miracle. Throughout Loren's illness our prayers of "a complete healing" were prayed over and over again, not just by us, but many others. Were our prayers answered? Oh most certainly. You see, Loren IS completely healed. He has a glorious new life ... and so do I. I am choosing to look at my life in that way. I have witnessed an incredible "shift in perception" in myself in this time since his diagnosis and in this time since he went HOME.

In these months I have rarely dreamt of Loren. But there he was last night. As has been the case in the few dreams I have had

I know he is here, I know it, but true to how he was in life ... there were few words spoken. I believe he was there last night to let me know, "Yes Hummies (what he called me), spot on. Miracles are a "shift in perception", and our miracle is the journey of love and growth that we took together and the growth that is continuing on in you."

Recognizing that each day we open our eyes and walk out into this world is a gift to each of us is a huge "shift in perception." You and me? We are as much a miracle as any "cure" can be. Thankful for the miracle of this life HE has given to me. And the NEW life Loren has been given. And the gift of knowing I am NEVER ALONE.

*****

The waves of emotion come over me at times least expected and the lack of emotion at other times I find surprising when not there. After speaking with my realtor this evening, a date has been chosen to put my house up for sale. Monday. Although I am praying, and ask for your prayers as well, that it happens to sell quickly I am also dreading that day. The day I sit in an office and sign away the place that I have lived the longest in my life. The place that was planned and built with the man that I have loved more than half of my life. The place where we raised our children and where our grandchildren came to know their Papa and Lala. I have thought about that day so many times in the last couple of months since deciding to go in that direction, praying that God would give me the strength and peace that I need as well as the guidance. Most times I feel HIS peace, especially when I walk through the doors of my "new home". But when I am here, when I sit in the quiet of this place, the depth of sadness is overwhelming.

So I pray that this happens quickly because for it to drag on would be much like what I experienced in those last few weeks of Loren's life. Knowing what was ahead but not knowing how long we would endure this time together. Excruciating ... all the while keeping a smile on my face and that brave exterior ... excruciating. I am beginning to feel that one can only experience so much of this without crumbling. I am growing weary from the pain and sadness ... and trying to remember that I am NEVER ALONE becomes harder with each passing day.

*****

"Because You have been my help, therefore in the shadow of Your wings I will rejoice. My soul follows close behind You; Your right hand upholds me".

Psalm 63:7-8

Today's devotion speaks of trusting God through all the turmoil, and that our inner peace need not be disturbed if our eyes focus on HIM and all that HE promises to us.

I know that if I read my journal from one year ago this day that this devotion from today would have been one that touched me deeply, but for totally different reasons. Loren had just had a major recurrence and was undergoing very harsh chemo. The anxiety was palpable, and I recall that there was a morning during that time I was literally brought to my knees in anguish with what my husband had been enduring. What we both had been enduring in our life together.

It was the first time that I began to feel that his journey was that he would be going to The Father, that I would be left here alone, and I was terrified. There was no peace for me at that time. And I am not feeling much peace now. I try so hard to feel the peace that HE wants for us. And after reading today's devotion I am reminded once again that HE is here, even when I can't feel HIM, watching over me, guiding me, blessing each moment of my day so that my heart and mind can find what is meant for each of us ... Peace. Praying to remember that today and that I am NEVER ALONE.

*****

It has been more than a month since I have treated myself to some ESC, otherwise known as "extreme self-care." Through counseling I have learned that it is essential to someone who is grieving to take very good care of themselves. Healing takes place in the present moment, so it is very necessary to take care of yourself not just emotionally, and spiritually, but physically as well. If healing takes place in the present moment than my attempt at extreme self-care today was an epic failure. I stopped to treat myself to a wonderful manicure and pedicure. While there they played non-stop Bee Gees and Carpenters songs. Try as I might I could not stay "in the present moment". So many memories began flooding my brain ... It seemed the words to each song brought tears to my eyes. The rollercoaster known as "grief". Some days we feel as if we can conquer the world and in the next moment ... nothing like trying to keep it together when your nails are drying.

*****

Today I was sitting here watching the History Channel and a commercial break talking about an upcoming documentary about 9/11 came on. Fifteen Septembers later. Fifteen. I can remember exactly where I was and what I was doing that morning when the unimaginable happened. I am quite certain most of us can. We were all horrified by the events of that day and I cannot imagine what it was like for those in our country that lived and worked closest to the events of that day, and those that had family and friends who did not come home.

All day on September 11th fifteen years ago and for days later, Loren and I watched the reports on the television. Loren began to have nightmares so I told him we would not watch anymore news reports, especially right before going to sleep at night.

As I sat here watching the commercial many memories came flooding back. All the fear for family, for friends, and for our country. And then this thought ..."The person I love more than anyone else in the world will never, ever have to witness another unimaginable, horrific act like we all witnessed on September 11th again. Ever. He is HOME where there is only peace. That brings me an incredible amount of comfort. One more "shift in perception."

*****

The home that we built from the ground up. The home that this December we would have shared for twenty-nine years. Monday is the day that I will begin to say goodbye to it. Strangers will walk through it ... it is my hope that they feel the love and care that has been in it for all of these years by a man who loved and supported his family and provided everything for them. A safe haven of love and protection. Most of all love. Praying the sale happens quickly because being here alone in this quiet, and empty place is so very sad ... and I try so hard to remember that I am truly NEVER ALONE.

~

September 2015

~

*****

"I will praise You, O Lord, with my whole heart;
I will tell of all Your marvelous works."
Psalm 9:1

Twenty-nine years ago today Loren and I stood at the top of our property and watched the bulldozers start clearing it to begin building what we considered to be our "forever home". We were so excited. Every hope and every dream for our family was going to be here in this place. We loved and respected this gift we had been given.

Today I will sign the papers to put our home up for sale. Although Loren will not be by my side physically, I know he has walked with me in these past weeks as I have prepared to say goodbye. "Forever" was not to be. I still cannot wrap my brain around that. Or that "home" will now be one without him. But, as thankful as we were September 4th twenty-nine years ago, I am now. And I never want to lose sight of all that we had been given by God then and Loren's hard work and God given talents that helped provide a beautiful life for us here and that he is providing for me now. Although I am finding it hard to be open to it at this moment, I am thankful, I am grateful and yes, I am blessed. I will find joy in this day for I am NEVER ALONE.

*****

Today has been a pretty amazing day. The first showing of the house has been very promising. It sounds as if they plan to send an offer. The house was shown again at 3:30 but I have not heard any feedback yet. It was supposed to be shown again this evening, but the person could not get off of work. Another showing is set up for tomorrow. I am feeling encouraged.

I have shared with a few people that for the first time since Loren died, which is almost five months now ... how is that possible ... that he feels so very present to me. I feel him here, and I can hear him saying "It's okay honey, I've got this. I am here beside you and I have been having conversations with our Father. We know how very hard this is for you. We are watching over you and HE is guiding this process. TRUST HIM, just like we did through our journey together in this past year. TRUST HIM.

I will sweetheart, I will ... as I try to remember I am NEVER ALONE.

*****

Today I am thankful for so many things, as I try to remember to be EVERY day. Sometimes in the craziness of all that I am having to deal with emotionally, financially and legally I lose sight of God's hand guiding me through this maze of this thing called "life" and “grief”. Today HE has again showed me HIS GREATNESS.

This morning after only two days on the market I received a full price offer on the house! I was elated ... but then the elation as the day wore on turned to melancholy. I know that I have to do this, I do. But that doesn't take away the sadness of saying goodbye to the home I have known for almost thirty years.

As I prepare to go to sleep tonight my thoughts turn to thankfulness for so many things in my life. Thankful to God. It is HIS hand who has orchestrated this day! Thankful to HIM for the many gifts HE blessed Loren and me with all of our years together. Loren's job, which if you have never heard that story remind me to share it one day. Our homes that we shared during our life together and the care that Loren so lovingly gave each of them. He was always so grateful and such a good steward to the gifts God gave him. Thankful for my realtor, who has guided me with such kindness through the purchase of my condo and the selling of my home. He has fully understood how difficult and how tender this time has been and he has always shown the utmost care and respect throughout this process. And once again, for all of you who have been here praying me through this journey. It has been an emotional and exhausting couple of months, and I am certain it will not be any easier as I move forward. So I ask your continued prayers. Love and thanks to God, to Loren and to all of you!

*****

Last night for an hour or so was a difficult and interesting time. God once again reminded me that HE is ALWAYS here in the midst of all the anxiety, HE is ALWAYS here. HE reminds me in subtle, but joyous ways. At around 8:30 I received a phone call from my realtor. He shared with me why, as I had suspected, there had not been an inspection done on my house today. The buyers had had a change of heart.

As you might imagine, I was not in a good place hearing that news. I was sitting there trying so hard not to fall apart. I was trying to have that "stiff upper lip" I have tried to maintain throughout the past year and a half of my life. Then the phone rang. It was a good friend I had not spoken with for a few weeks. It is always great talking to him. I refer to him as my “brother from another mother”. We always have good laughs, but last night’s phone call was a bit different. I am still trying to discern whether he saw my post and that that is what prompted his phone call, or if it was a God thing? Nudging someone who cares about me to reach out at that moment when it was so needed. He asked me how I was, and it was one of the rare times I did not lie and say, "I'm okay". I told him, "I've been better" and I shared what I had just learned on the phone call with my realtor. He said he was sorry and that I was doing such a great job with "everything" and that he would not be able to do what I have been doing. The flood gates opened. The reality is, what choice do we have? The way I look at it is we have two choices. We can push through it all. Dig down deep inside AND raise our hands up to HIM to carry us through, or we can curl up into a fetal position and stop living life. I think I have been doing a pretty good job of digging down deep, but I often do not feel like I am "living" life. I often feel like I am a spectator while "life" just keeps passing me by. I wonder when I will begin to feel like I am living life again.

I am so thankful for my friend's phone call. In the end, like always, he had me laughing. laughing always feels so healing. Yes, it was most definitely a "God thing"... HE knew what my heart needed at that moment.

After that phone call I saw a message under my post from my friend Jeff. Psalm 20:7. Reminding me of WHOM I needed to place my trust. Our Lord God.

I am thankful for both of these friends who have reminded me in very different ways to continue on. Live life and to remember to trust in HIM and know that I am NEVER ALONE.

*****

Today I spent the day "running". No, not "running" in the way that most people think of running ... but by "running away". Away from the hurt and the pain that began my day as I woke up once again with the realization that Loren is no longer physically here with me. Pain more deeply felt today as I move into a series of days between now and the first of the year of so many meaningful dates. My birthday, our anniversary, our grandchildren's birthdays ... three of them practically back-to-back. The upcoming holiday season which would have been Loren's 60th birthday. How in God's name am I supposed to get through it all? How do I keep "running" away from all of the pain?

The day started with pampering myself. From there I drove to a shopping center about a half an hour from here. With every step I took I imagined Loren beside me. "Oh look honey, there is a wallet like yours that fell apart last week. Let me get you that for your birthday ... Oh, let's go into Yankee Candle! You can get some new "Fall Crispy" scents that you always love this time of year"... everywhere I went he was there. And then there was our church celebration tonight. The 50th anniversary of the first Mass. It was a conversation Loren had numerous times during the year of his illness. He was going to get well, and he was going to help our social director by setting up and cleaning up the celebration. He was always there helping during our gatherings at church, and he planned to be there for this. That was not to be.

Do I run TO or do I run AWAY from this? I chose to run TO ...

I did "fine" I suppose, although there was constant thought that Loren should be there tonight standing next to me. And then it hit me with all the emotion I had been running from all day. It was time for receiving the Eucharist and the music began. "I Am The Bread of Life". It only took singing the first line and the tears came. I knelt there trying to pull myself together when a woman sitting next to me, who I didn't know, reached across and just kept saying, "It is HIS will, it is HIS will." All I could do was nod my head. I needed that reminder. I needed to remember that all that has transpired in this last year is HIS will. HIS journey for Loren and HIS journey for me. As I received communion, Father John reached out hugged me and it took me back to that moment at Loren's funeral when the sorrow was almost too much to bear. I wonder if I will ever be able to hear that song again without falling apart. The words being the very depth of Loren's faith in his Lord and Savior.

"I'm broken and it hurts Father"... I wonder, will it forever feel like this? I know that these next months will be even more difficult than the last have been. I know that the only thing that will sustain me is to continue to remember that it is HIS will, and it is HIM who will continue to give me strength, hope and courage.

Tonight was a beautiful Fall evening. The heat and the humidity have dissipated. I feel refreshed ... at this moment I feel renewed ... is it the weather, or is it the reminder from a stranger? It is HIS will ... and I am NEVER ALONE.

*****

The saying "grief comes in waves" is so true. You go along each day "living" your life or trying your best to and without warning you see something or hear something or experience something that sets off a tidal wave of emotion. Sometimes, it doesn't take anything at all. Perhaps it's just the emotional fatigue of grief. That's more often how it is for me.

Last night was one of those times for me. I climbed into bed and reached for my evening prayers and once I had prayed I laid down and reached for the cross that Loren had been given by someone from our church and that he always had with him throughout his chemo treatments. I go to sleep each night with it in my hand. As I laid there last night the tidal wave began. Overwhelmed with trying to continue the balance of work and all that is ahead of me with trying to sell the house and feeling pulled between my two homes I continued to pray and cry out to God. The "whys" and the "I don't understands" of the journey that HE has put in front of me became too much as I laid there in the dark. But as quickly as the tidal wave swept in it receded. I found myself being thankful, realizing all the good that HE has given me in the midst of everything. I asked HIM for HIS love and HIS guidance and for a peaceful night's rest. Before I knew it my alarm was going off.

When I read the days devotional I was reminded once again that HE is ALWAYS here beside me, listening and loving me through it all ... HE is my "strength and my song"... and I am NEVER ALONE.

~

October

2015

~

*****

Today was a good day. A day when I was reminded that HE is always here with me and has put wonderful people in my life to show me HIS presence. I decided I needed a bit of joy today, so I went to a craft fair in Gay, Georgia and met my friend Jodi and her son there. We had a very enjoyable time, and it was definitely a change of pace for my weary mind and body.

Afterward I went home and loaded more boxes and other belongings in the car as next weekend will be moving day ... and so much more. I am trying my best to stay busy ... later my friend Jeff came with a couple of his friends to do another enormous task for me. They moved my washer and dryer to my new home. It was no easy task for sure. I am always struck by these incredible people. Nothing is too much or too big, and it is always as though it is no big deal. I imagine that is because they are filled with the Holy Spirit and because of that they are humble and kind and nothing is too much for them to handle. After Jeff and I finished another task, I went back and unloaded my car and put some of those things away. It was almost 10:00PM when I left there to come "home"... I feel confused when I say the word “home” as I'm not really sure where that is right now. I am so very thankful to Jeff and his friends and to God. GOD IS SO VERY GOOD and THANK YOU for the wonderful servants you gifted me with today! My heart is full of gratitude.

I am NEVER ALONE.

*****

Today has been a difficult day ... at least the later part of it.

People say when you are going through a difficult time that you should stay in the moment, live only each hour as they come and not think too far ahead. Honestly, I feel I have done better when I think ahead. But as this week has loomed in front of me I have felt distracted, often times that I am having an "out of body" experience.

For some reason I had not realized what the date was. I have been so fixated on Saturday as that will be "moving day" and on Sunday the 11th which would have been our 35th wedding anniversary. Thinking of that anniversary coming is almost too much at times ... but what has happened in the last few hours has almost been as well.

Late this morning after my friend and co-worker had picked up the children from lunch she did calendar time with them. As I worked at my desk she began by saying "Today is Thursday October 8th". Where had my mind been all day and why was I just realizing today was the 8th of the month? It has been SIX months since Loren has died. I most certainly had thought about Loren today ... many, many times, but I had not realized the significance of the day. After that moment I was just trying to get through the rest of the day at work.

*****

Two of my sons arrived at the house today to get a number of things. One in a U-Haul the other with a friend in a truck. Removing these things that Loren and I had purchased to make our house a "home" for our family to come "home" to ... and now there are just empty rooms. The echo throughout the house that I have heard for months even more pronounced. Now there is no Loren and there is no family and there is no home to come home to. My one son left, unceremoniously, the other left handing me his house key and saying as he did "I guess this is the last time I will be in this house". I was speechless with emotion and all I could do was nod my head and say "yes, it is". He drove away. I couldn't even watch. I walked back inside, cried and grabbed my car keys.

For the first time in my life I am out in public ... alone ... drinking ... is that a bad thing? I don't know, but right now I don't really give a crap.

*****

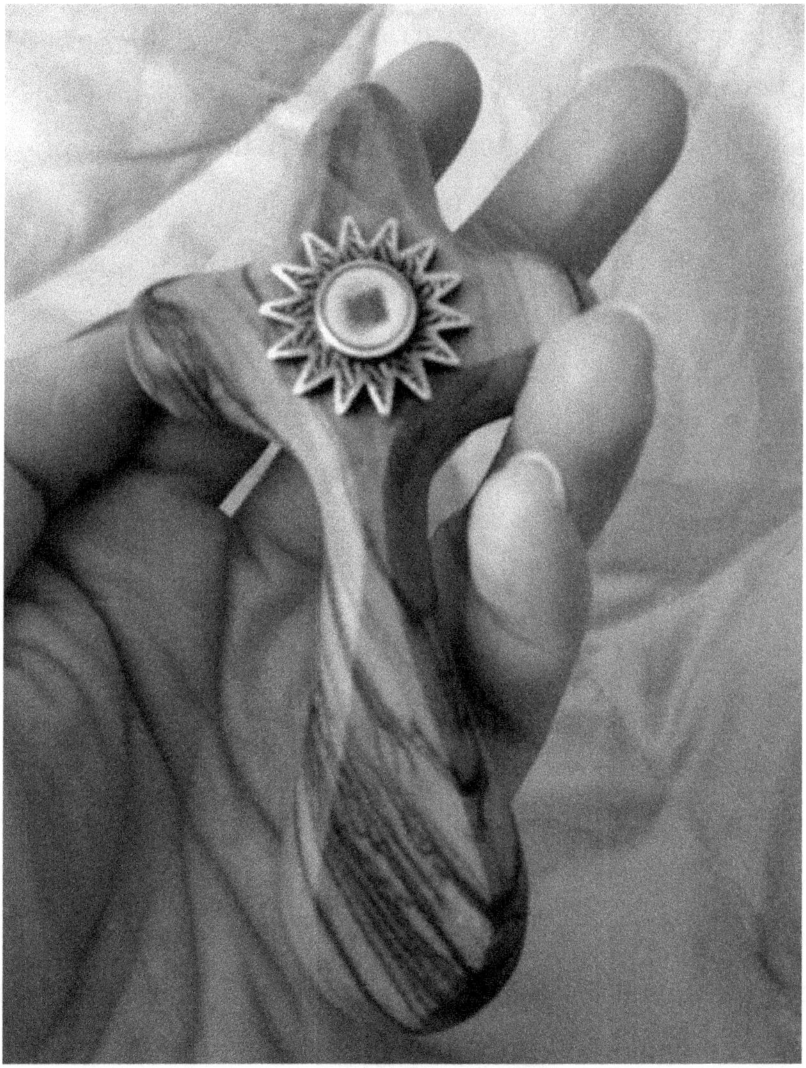

This is a very special cross.

Loren was given this cross one Sunday morning after mass after being anointed with many church members present. He was told by the woman who gave it to him that it is called a Jerusalem cross and is made from wood from the Holy Land. It is quite beautiful, and Loren carried it with him daily and always made sure that it was with him when he was in the hospital having his chemo treatments. Holding it in his hand and praying while doing so gave him great peace. Somehow between his last hospital stay and going to hospice it got "misplaced." After he passed I was beside myself when I couldn't find it. When I began going through his things, I found it in the small pocket of the suitcase he had with him his last hospital stay. To say I was overjoyed when I found it is an understatement. In fact I began to cry. To be able to hold this cross in my hand knowing how much it meant to Loren and how often he had gained such comfort from it ... there are no words.

Since the day I found it I have held it in my hand every night as I have gone to sleep. I hold it when I pray, and I hold it when I am finding it hard to find the words to say to HIM. HE knows what is there in my heart, and I know that is all that matters. Today I used this cross much in the way that Loren did through his year long journey. I put it in my pocket and throughout the day when I felt my emotions might overtake me, I would reach into my pocket and put my hand around it asking God and Loren to give me the strength and the peace to move forward in the journey. And that will be my prayer tonight, with this cross tight in my hand, I will hold tight to what it is HE has me moving toward ... whatever that may be, and I will remember that I am NEVER ALONE.

*****

Thirty-five years ago today I married the most extraordinary man. A man who loved, respected, protected and provided for me and our family without question or hesitation. Only his devotion to God came before me or his family. My heart has ached non-stop since the day his ceased. Especially in this last week as the time was closing in on the day I would leave the home we shared for almost 29 years. Today, in this moment that I have chosen to sit in this space and take time to breathe and to relax I am remembering his love, the provider and the protector he was and has continued to be for me. I love you sweetheart, thank you for the thirty-four and a half years you gave of yourself to me and to your family.

*****

Today was a long day ... work, grocery shopping, and then I returned to the house to clean up the lawn. Blowing leaves ... quite a chore on the one-and-a-half-acre wooded property. Although yard work is something I truly don't enjoy today I found myself lost in thought to the drone of the blower. Finishing the front I moved around to the backyard and as the late afternoon Autumn sunlight dappled through the trees so many memories came flooding back. This memory was one of them. This precious tender moment between a grandfather and his first grandchild.

I captured this moment that afternoon and I am so blessed that I did. This man adored this little boy and this little boy adored his Papa. How can one memory make you both happy and sad at the same time? I guess grief is like that.

*****

"Joy Comes Again"... this morning I am listening to music that touches my heart, and this is the name of the song that is playing. As I am listening I am wondering ... when will "Joy come again"? ... I have a hard time finding the joy, but often when I talk to my friend Celeste she will say "see, you just found the "JOY" in your day." I feel so blessed to have people in my life who help remind me of that when I have a hard time seeing it for myself. As I sit here listening to "Joy Comes Again" on this gorgeous Autumn morning I promise that I will look for that joy ... today and every day.

*****

A beautiful and touching evening of music tonight. I was so fortunate to be able to spend time talking to William Ackerman and Stanton Lanier two incredibly talented musicians. William Ackerman is the founder of Windham Hill Records and the music that he has composed and produced has been part of my life since I was in my late teens. My mother loved the music from the Windham Hill artists, and I have carried that love of hers with me through the years. It has remained a huge part of my life all these years but never more so than the last year when it would be with Loren and myself through hospital stays, at home in bed at rest and at prayer and it was with us in the hospice as Loren made his transition from this place to his Heavenly Father. How blessed I was to share this with these two men tonight and for William to share his story on stage when he began playing "The Impending Death of The Virgin Spirit" which he wrote about his mother and then spoke of the conversation we had before the concert began. This is why his music touches people the way that it does because he is so touched by the stories that are shared with him of what his music has meant to our lives. Thankful to my friend Tricia who was my "chariot" tonight and shared this beautiful experience with me.

*****

The past twenty-four hours has been a time when I have been reminded of the gifts of others. The gift of giving without thought of getting anything back in return. My eyes have been blind to that for some months now with the darkness of grief that covers my eyes. The beauty of music that I have known for a lifetime shared with others last night was an experience I won't soon forget.

This morning I arrived at work to the sound of Christmas music playing (yes, it's the 25th of the month) and delicious treats, all homemade, by a beautiful lady who keeps Christmas in her heart all year long. She gives so much of herself to others

... individually and collectively, never with a thought of "getting" in return.

Then I walked into my classroom to a lovely surprise sitting on my desk. Roses. Pink roses which have deep meaning for me from my friend who went to the concert with me last night. And then there is my co-worker and friend who brings joy and laughter to me every day in so many ways. God knows how my heart has been aching ... on the outside I hear, "You're doing so good"... I know differently. Today HE has reminded me that the life HE has planned for me, the journey HE has me on is good. As my sister reminds me often, "God is good"... there is good in every day, but for me the "good" has been "exceptional" in the past twenty-four hours. To all of you who have answered HIS call and reached out, God Bless. I am reminded I am NEVER ALONE.

~

November 2015

~

"And God will wipe away every tear from their eyes;
There shall be no more death, nor sorrow, nor crying.
There shall be no more pain, for the former things have passed away."
Revelation 21:4

*****

Today began at 4AM when I woke and couldn't go back to sleep until, of course, right before my alarm went off at 5:00. When I woke at 4AM my mind raced with so many thoughts. I reached for my phone which I imagine most of us have a bad habit of doing when we can't sleep. It was then I saw the news of another loss for our school family. My heart was so heavy with thoughts and prayers of her and for her family because I know the sorrow that they are feeling, and I searched for "the right words" to share with her daughter who worked at our school and her family. As I shared with several of my school "family" members today, it doesn't matter that you have experienced this deep loss, you still feel as though there are no words adequate enough that will "help" with the sorrow someone feels at the loss of their loved one.

I have shared so many times how I believe with all my heart that I was led to this place, this "home", this "family" by God's hand because HE knows all of our needs long before we know the circumstances that arise in our lives. HE knew where I would need to be and the love and support that would be needed in my life. A place where HIS love shines through so many of the people I come into contact with each day.

Today was one of those days, from beginning to end. From Jeff who has helped me in so many ways and others who have encouraged me to put my feet on the floor and put one foot in front of the other each day. Even though our sorrow was for another today, they were HIS eyes and HIS arms reaching out to me because they know that this experience for our "family" rips open a wound for me that still runs deep. I was touched deeply by each embrace and each "are you okay"? I would respond with a nod of my head or a "yes thank you so much" I would walk away with tears in my eyes and a "thank you Lord Jesus" on my lips for this "home" that HE placed me in five years ago.

Later in the day one of our precious ladies asked if we would like to meet at a local restaurant to share conversation and yes, grieve ... together. After a number of ladies left the gathering the few of us that were left sat talking and the conversation turned to the last days, hours and minutes that I had with Loren. I am thankful for these friends, these "family" members who sat and listened and allowed me to share with them, allowed me to grieve with them. For it is in the telling of our story that we begin to heal, and I have found for many months now that many people do not want to hear it. They do not want you to tell your "story". They talk around and about "it" and you can see in their eyes that they hope and pray that you don't bring "it" up. I have figured out the "why" to that. It is too painful. It brings a reality to their lives that they just don't want to "see". But the lesson that needs to be learned is that it is in the sharing of our stories, the sharing of our grief that allows healing to take place.

On the eighth it will be seven months since Loren's death. My "story" has been stifled. There hasn't been enough of the "story-telling" to allow the healing process to take place...to really begin. Even my mother whose husband has died has said that "no one wants to hear your story". At first I didn't want to believe that, but I believe she may be right.

So, to my precious "family" members, thank you for allowing HIS light to shine through your eyes and thank you for allowing me to share my "story" ... Loren's "story"... our "story". I love you and thank you.

*****

They say, "out of the mouth of babes". Today as the children were gathered to be told of their beloved music teachers' death the term "passed away" was used. When asked if anyone knew what that meant their little hands went up and several of them gave an answer. One little girl said, "It means that she started a new chapter". I think we were all taken aback by the answer.

As I get ready for bed this evening I will reflect on that response. Maybe it will take some of the pain away from my loss, and for others if we could just think of that ... a "new chapter begins" for those we love who have gone to live the promise we have all been given. Eternal Life ... the new chapter. Amen to that! Love and prayers for peace and comfort for all who need it tonight.

*****

It's official. I had been holding my breath after hearing many stories from people of buyer's loans falling through. But I received a text from my realtor this afternoon. The buyer's loan has been fully approved.

Since moving into my new home a month ago I have gone over to the house frequently to check on it. When I went over a few days ago I walked through the house ... dark and empty ... just the echo of my footsteps ... and I thought to myself "how sad". How sad that the man who had worked so hard all of his life for this home is gone and with him the family that he loved so dearly. Walking from room to room I recalled the first days in December so many years ago on a day just like this day I was there ... rainy and gloomy ... but how the weather couldn't dampen our excitement or happiness to be in our "forever home". I felt oddly non-emotional. Empty. Much like the house.

Tuesday I will be sitting at a table alone with a stranger who walked into our home and decided that he wanted to make it his. I'm not sure how I am going to feel when that happens. How will I feel when I begin signing my name to the papers that will make it his when all those years ago there were two signatures on those papers and now there will be only one? How can that be? How can everything Loren did for his family be gone with the stroke of a pen and only my signature? I truly don't know how that is going to feel. I think I am going to have to be praying about this ... a lot ... and praying that I will know I am NEVER ALONE.

*****

This morning I am sitting here in, as I like to refer to, my little cocoon. A place that is warm and a place where I feel safe. My new home.

I am thankful for that warmth that I feel is Loren's loving heart and arms surrounding me. I am thankful for the peacefulness that envelops me when I am here and for the peacefulness that God has placed in my heart, as I have been very prayerful asking HIM for that. I am thankful for HIS gifts to Loren and to me all these years and for the gifts that HE continues to give me now.

I believe that words and prayers have power. I do. So I will choose to hold in my heart as the holiday season begins in all its beauty these words, "love, peace, joy, blessed and thankful." I am blessed to have known the love of an extraordinary man. I am joyful at the life we shared together. I am Thankful for the peacefulness that I was able to have in my life because of my life with him, and I am thankful to God for bringing him into my life all those years ago and for blessing our life together. Thankful, grateful and blessed. My powerful words.

*****

I went for a short visit to Oklahoma to visit Marie and Michael. I arrived home from OKC around noon today and I decided while I was feeling it I would begin decorating for Christmas. A couple of years ago Loren bought me a new star for Christmas for the top of the tree. This year I just couldn't put that star on top of the tree. I thought it more fitting to put the star that Loren and I bought with the money that his grandparents gave to us for Christmas the first year we were married. I love that old star ... or shall I say "vintage" star? Yes, it's just perfect.

*****

Tomorrow it will be eight months that I "gave him back". Gave him back to The One who he had lived his whole life for. Yes, that moment was hard, but living these past eight months without him has been harder.

Last night I had dinner with an old friend. Someone I haven't seen in several years. Someone who didn't know about Loren's illness or his death until after. She loved Loren, respected him, and knew how blessed my life was with him in it. We spent hours together last night and I shared our journey and mine since he went home. She looked at me at one point during the evening and asked me, "so, how are you doing"? I told her I wasn't certain. I told her that perhaps other people could be a better judge of that than I could. Truth is there are times I feel I could take on the world and "win" if there is such a thing. But that at other times I feel that I would like to walk to the edge of a big black hole and be sucked into the abyss.

The reality is that I know neither of those two things will happen and I know that my life will never be the same since I "gave him back". One thing I do know is that to honor Loren I will continue to walk this journey and be obedient to HIS will, as Loren was to HIM. When I allow myself to close my eyes and "see" those last moments again I know that I will never forget them, and I know that I was so blessed to have had them ... those moments when for the first time in his life he left me ... he went HOME ... I "gave him back". I was strong enough to TELL him to go. It was probably the most unselfish thing I have ever done in my life. I told my friend last night if there was one thing I ever felt I could be proud of myself for, it was in that moment. The moment I "gave him back"... and doing my best to remember I am NEVER ALONE.

~

December

2015

~

"My brethren, count it all joy when you fall into
Various trials, knowing that the testing of your faith
Produces patience. But let patience have its perfect work,
that you may be perfect and complete, lacking nothing."
James 1:2-4

*****

This morning I was sharing with a friend at work my happiness about beginning an online grief program this evening. As we were talking she said, "I want to ask you something. Do you prefer people to speak of Loren in the past or present tense"? I was stunned by the question. I had not really thought about that, but my response was easy. I shared that I have not even been able to form an opinion about that because frankly, hardly anyone even speaks about him. Is that others experience as well? I always wonder about that.

*****

I am often amazed at how acquaintances deem it okay to tell you not only where you should be in your grief journey, but WHO you should be in your grief journey. I not only am not WHO I was when I began this journey during Loren's illness, I may not be who I was yesterday. My face, the face of grief changes from one day to the next ... sometimes from one moment to the next.

I will not "get over it" and it doesn't "get better." It changes over time. Each day is a learning experience as to how I will "get through it." Walk with me if you choose to, but do not criticize what you do not understand ... me, or anyone else living with the death of someone they love. Today I am not feeling the "grace".

*****

I have come to realize that it is very important to live "intentionally" My intention is to continue to believe in the inner strength I found in myself while walking the year long journey of Loren's illness and the 8 months since his death. An inner strength that I never knew existed in me. I know that Loren saw it in me and I want to make him proud of me and honor our relationship by living the life he would want me to.

I am grateful ~

Today I am grateful to have had an extraordinary man in my life who loved me unconditionally for 34 years. I am grateful for the home that Loren and Our Father provided for me and for our family and for the new home they have provided for me now. A home where I feel safe, warm, comfortable and happy. I am grateful to God whose hand has put me in a place where I have been loved and supported through the difficult journey of the past year and a half. I am grateful for my co-worker who makes me LAUGH EVERY DAY!!! and I am grateful for the new found strength and belief in myself.

*****

This morning as I lay here looking out the window as the sun begins to rise my attention has been on a barren tree. I am struck by my own thoughts about it. I am thinking that I could choose to look at my life like this tree ... barren and lifeless, or I could choose to remember that my life, like this tree will be full. Full of life once again. That MY journey here continues ... I am grateful for this tree in all its barren beauty teaching me a lesson on this beautiful Sunday morning.

*****

This week I began an online grief group to help those who are grieving through the holiday season. The past couple of days there has been a lot of focus on gratitude, even for the smallest of things.

This morning I am grateful for this quiet moment that I can sit in this space and enjoy the memories of Loren's gift to me many years ago. "Jolly" and "Joy" mugs that I had seen at Starbucks. He couldn't surprise me often, but he did that Christmas! I have loved them for so many years, but most especially now. This morning I choose "JOY". Grateful.

*****

Today I'm grateful to my son Matt who came to visit with my two grandsons even though his life is in chaos right now. I so miss these two little guys. Logan, who is four, was our first grandchild and the apple of his Papa's eye. Logan adored his Papa and his Papa adored him. My heart aches every time I think of how the two of them were together. Today Logan gathered the set of decorative Christmas trees together that are sitting on the end table. He said "Look Lala, here is Papa and Daddy and Lala and Logan and Ollie and we are all holding hands in a circle. We need to put something in the middle Lala." I told him "I have just the perfect thing Logan." We put a candle in the middle. He said, "That's perfect Lala." Be still my heart. I wanted to burst out crying. Heartbroken ...

*****

> Tears have a wisdom all their own. They come when a person has relaxed enough to let go and to work through his sorrow. They are the natural bleeding of an emotional wound, carrying the poison out of the system. Here lies the road to recovery.
> F. Alexander Magoun

Sometime shortly after Loren's death I found this quote online. Today I was given the gift of releasing those "poisons" from my emotional wounds and I am so thankful for that ... now to practice breathing and taking care of myself. Grateful, thankful, blessed.

*****

I am in my fourth day of my grief program. I am finding it to be uplifting, life giving but most of all TRANSFORMING ... I am learning that it's okay to give myself permission to be happy. It's hard, especially this time of year to be happy and joy filled when you are living with the death of a loved one, but I am committed to wanting them for myself. To "transform" my pain and sorrow into remembering, loving and honoring the man Loren was to me and to his family and all those who knew him.

*****

I am sitting here tonight quietly reflecting once again on time online with the grief group. I'm taking time to remember so many beautiful joy-filled memories. How in the world could I possibly not have thought of this moment! The weekend Loren and I first met. My brother's wedding in August of 1978. I was barely out of high school. My brother was in the Air Force at the time. Loren decided to re-enlist for a fifth year and was sent to KI Sawyer AFB in the upper peninsula of MI where my brother was stationed. They became good friends, and he came home with my brother the weekend he got married.

I knew by the end of that four days he was in Ohio that this was the man I was going to spend the rest of my life with. The "rest of MY life" was not to be, but how honored, how blessed, how privileged I am that he spent the rest of HIS life with me. What a precious, precious memory this is. I am grateful to have spent this time reflecting and putting these memories back where they belong ... into my heart to embrace and hold dear and to remember the love.

*****

This is a picture from my fiftieth birthday and our thirtieth wedding anniversary gathering at our home in September 2010.

What I am choosing to remember about Loren today is how he lived his life, which was completely unselfishly. I am a huge fan of contemporary jazz music, especially guitar. I happened to have seen that a favorite guitarist did "living room concerts". I asked Loren if he had been thinking about doing anything for my fiftieth birthday and he said, "well I was thinking about it". Lol, I knew my husband well enough to know that really he had not, but I was going for it. I told him I would like to look into having a living room concert and we could combine the celebration with our thirtieth wedding anniversary in October. Being who he was he said absolutely I could check on that. Yes, I actually planned my own party. I had never had a birthday party, so I was going to do it up big!

It was an amazing night, and I will never forget how Loren was only concerned about my happiness leading up to and including that special night. But his whole life was about that as far as myself and our children were concerned. What a blessing to have been loved by a man who was so unselfish.

*****

Participating in a grief program is hard work. It is emotional and draining, but it forces you to confront the painful things that often times stay suppressed because no one wants to hear your pain. No one allows you to share the painful things that will allow the healing to begin. Today we were asked to share a word or words that describe how we are feeling at this time. One word that comes to mind is "lonely". The workplace is great. It takes a lot of energy and I am surrounded by so many fun and energetic people. However, when it is time for a break everyone sprints out the door and is off to parts unknown and I feel like I am left standing there while everyone just dissipates into thin air.

Friday will be our last day at work before Christmas and I've already been listening to everyone talk about what they are doing. Loren worked in the airline industry for years, we were transplants to the Atlanta area and so besides our children, neither one of us has family here. We "made our family". Church, work and neighbors ... all ever changing because so many would come and go.

Our family fell apart in this last year and I know that this Christmas will not be one of family and tradition, although my daughter and son-in-law will be coming in for just a couple of days. Having spent time thinking of this I have often thought that I would love to get on a plane and fly anywhere ... anywhere at all.

*****

It is so funny, okay maybe funny is not the right word to use ... but when you have a clear intention to live and think happy, and joyful thoughts, how wonderful memories about those we love who have died just come unexpectedly! I have no idea why THIS memory popped into my head this morning as I was driving to work, but it made me laugh out loud when it did! I would bake dozens and dozens of cookies at the holidays and my “snowball” cookies loaded with powdered sugar were Loren's favorites. Every year without fail he would go to take that first bite and inevitably he would inhale as he did sucking the powdered sugar in and choking! EVERY year! Makes me smile! Great way to begin my day!

*****

I saw this quote online today and I wanted to cry when I read it. As lonely, as heartbreaking and as sorrowful as some moments can be I KNOW that what I have experienced in the past year and a half of my life has changed me ... for the better, and that every day when my feet hit the floor, I am rebuilding my life, my spirit, my soul. I am being obedient to The Father because THIS is the journey HE has put in front of me, and I WILL walk it. It is not always easy, but I can see what it is doing for me. It has changed me; I have realized so many things about myself. Mostly that I AM HEALING ... that I WANT TO ... and most of all, I WANT TO LIVE ... because Loren wants me to and because God wants me to!

> "...There are times when we will experience heartbreaking sorrow, when we will grieve and when we may be tested to our limits. However, such difficulties allow us to change for the better, to rebuild our lives in the way our Heavenly Father teaches us, and to become something different from what we were — better than what we were, more understanding than what we were, more empathetic than what we were, with stronger testimonies than we had before."
>
> -Thomas S. Monson
> October 2013

*****

I'm curious. Does anyone else go out to eat by themselves? I'm sitting here in a Thai restaurant ... a nice restaurant that Loren and I only went to a few times ... for special occasions. I have decided that EVERY day of my life is now a special occasion. And while it does sometimes sting to look around me and see so many couples having conversations, that I often find myself wondering what they may be about and longing for that companionship, I know that I have to do these things. I can't just sit at home and not go out into this world and enjoy it. Mmmm, cashew nut chicken just arrived. It smells delicious!

*****

Like so many people my life has had an enormous amount of loss in the past two years. Tomorrow will be our last day at school before Christmas break so this morning when I woke, I decided to take the time to write a letter of thanks and gratitude to two people who have been so important to me in this journey of the past year and a half. The "theme", if you will, was just this, that "life is a gift", and that they have most definitely been a gift in my life. My heart feels so good this morning sharing this with them ... I am ready to start my day, it is a gift ... and I am so thankful for that.

*****

From the beginning of Loren's illness he was prayed over by so many. We prayed and prayed and prayed that God would bring to us the miracle of a cure for his cancer.

I have been asked many, many times if I am angry at God, after all there were so many prayers on Loren's behalf. No. Not at this moment. I have had brief moments of anger, but Loren and I lived throughout the year of his illness with the belief that our lives were in HIS hands and that whatever HIS will was for Loren and for me was what we would do our best to accept.

When we were told the month prior to Loren's death that there was nothing else medically that could be done for Loren I watched Loren surrender himself completely to God's will. He was at total peace and I was humbled to sit by his side every day for those last few weeks and watch him pray himself into HIS arms. I guess what I am saying is that I could sit and wonder WHY? WHY have others been cured of their illnesses? WHY have others suffered horrific accidents and lived? It's hard not to wonder that. I have done my best to stay in a place of understanding that we all have a journey, a purpose and when we have accomplished that journey, that purpose we go "HOME"... Loren went "HOME" exactly when he was supposed to. I will do my best to believe that forever.

*****

"On Eagles Wings" ~

I am sitting here on the computer looking through music and this piece ... this beautiful piece brings me right back to the last hours and minutes with Loren. Baring the soul time ... Loren's thoughts even to the end were always for me. The day before he died, I knew his death was close. He had had a few visitors that morning and after they left he fell asleep. I sat quietly next to him, stroking his arms, music was playing softly on my iPad. After a couple of hours he opened his eyes and looked at me and said, "Oh, you're still here." I smiled and said, "Of course I am honey." Then he said, "I'm so sorry for everything that I have put you through." I told him that he had nothing to be sorry for and that I would do it all over again if I could have more time with him. And then I said, "But I want you to promise me something." He said, "I will"..."I want you to promise me that when God holds out his hands to you that you will go to him" ... "I promise", he said.

After that he went back to sleep. Our pastor, Father John, came to the hospice and had Mass in the room and anointed Loren. After he left I went out to speak with the nun who was the charge nurse at the hospice and told her that I didn't want to go home that night. (They only allowed you to stay if they thought that death was imminent) She told me that she wanted me to remember something. She said that it may not be God's will for me to be there when Loren passed. WRONG! I looked her square in the face and said NO! That was NOT happening. That I had walked every step of that journey with Loren and that God WAS NOT TAKING HIM WITHOUT ME BY HIS SIDE! She was quite taken aback by my forcefulness, but she was going to have to get over it. But as we good Catholic girls do, I left but with a heavy heart. Before I left though I tried to get Loren to wake. It was very difficult, but I was not leaving before I heard him say, "I love you". He did, and as I walked out that door I knew it was going to be the last time I ever heard him speak those words to me.

I cried all the way home, calling my children and telling them that they needed to start preparing to come home, that I felt the time was close. For the first time in the two and a half weeks that he was in hospice I called all through the night to check on him and each time was told that he was resting peacefully. When I arrived in the morning it was obvious that he was making his transition. My heart was breaking but I knew that I had to continually give him permission to go HOME.

As the time grew closer I began to sing this hymn to him. One of our favorites. Every time I would reach the words ..."and hold you in the palms of HIS hands" I would stop and whisper to him "Do you see HIM honey, go to HIM, HE is waiting for you." As he took his last breaths, he opened his eyes and his mouth as if he were trying to speak. I have wished so many times that I knew what he was trying to say. My friend who was there says he was telling me he loved me and thanking me for giving him permission to go. Whenever I allow myself to think of these last moments of his life I want to believe that. And my pastor has told me that with the many, many times he has stood by someone's bedside with the family gathered around that those moments were the most beautiful that he had witnessed. How unselfish I was to have let Loren go with dignity and grace.

I pray that is what he felt in those moments. Thank you for letting me share my story ... I needed to tonight. Thank you.

*****

Today was a wonderful day. I started the morning with the intent to live joyfully ... it started with taking the time to write a letter to two friends who have walked this journey beside me with love, patience and kindness, and I wanted them to know what that has meant to me.

Then I treated my co-worker and myself to some Christmassy nails! Nail art! Living on the wild side! Libby has NEVER done nail art! Oh what JOY! A snowflake nail! Makes me happy and it made my co-worker happy as well!

When I came home a Christmas gift to my daughter had arrived. It fills me with happiness to be giving this gift to her. It is a book about learning to live with grief that I have found helpful. Loren was my husband, but she lost her Dad. The man that was EVERYTHING to her. I never want to be lost so deeply in grief to forget that she and my other children are walking this journey as well. Having received this book within a week of Loren's death and reading it shortly after receiving it I KNOW with my whole heart that it has been what has enabled me to look at not just Loren's death but his LIFE in such a different way. So different that at times I wonder if when I share my thoughts, my heart and my soul with family and friends if they wonder whether or not I "loved Loren enough"? I loved him with all of my heart, but I also want to honor him by LIVING joyfully.

*****

I can't believe I am going to share this, because I am not sure I have said this or thought this at all in the past eight months ... but today I feel as if I'm drowning. I feel as though the waves are crashing over top of me and I can't get my head up for air.

I left school this afternoon with a heavy heart and was holding back tears every time someone called after me and wished me a Merry Christmas. When I got home I went to the mailbox and there was a Christmas card from my Mom. My Dad died a year and a half ago. She wrote in her card that "our men are watching over us and are proud of who we've become." I burst into tears and have been crying ever since. How could this man who had taken such incredible care of himself be gone at fifty-nine years old? The 23rd Loren would have turned sixty years old. In the past week I had been thinking of how I would make him his favorite lemon meringue pie. That's what he requested last year as well. I was going to put some number candles on it and enjoy a piece of pie. I'm so angry and I want to take this computer and throw it through the freaking window right now! Yes, I am having one of my rare moments of anger at Loren's death.

I don't want to be like this, I don't want to feel like this. Loren was such a peaceful person. I don't like that all of this anger right now is because he is not here. The past 24 hours have been pretty emotional, probably the most emotional since the sale and closing on our home in November. I need to see that HUGE, sweet, precious smile right in front of me ... NOW, RIGHT NOW, and I need to try very hard to remember that I am NEVER ALONE.

*****

Yesterday was not a good day emotionally for me. I am taking the time today to take care of myself, starting with cooking myself breakfast. I have only "cooked" myself breakfast twice in the past eight months and it just occurred to me as I was doing it this morning why. Loren was the breakfast maker. He loved to make me breakfast on a Saturday morning and on Sundays when we came home from church. He made the best omelets! I have to take better care of myself.

*****

Several weeks ago I had a stomach bug. It was the first time I had been sick, literally since Loren had been diagnosed with cancer a year and a half ago. And I mean I was REALLY sick. I was up every hour during the night sick. All I could do was lay there all through the night thinking to myself, "So this is what it will be like not having Loren here by my side, through "sickness and in health" to not have that person here by my side who I matter so much to and would be my comfort and my strength during times of illness, like I was for him.

Since Loren died eight months ago I have had dreams where I knew he was there, but he was always "hazy". I knew he was there, but it always seemed that he was just out of reach. The night after I had been so sick I dreamt of Loren. Truthfully, I'm not sure it was a dream. It was so real that I literally gasped when I woke up. He spoke to me and he told me that he "was always with me". When I went back to sleep he came to me again. I won't forget that feeling of having him so near. He was here to remind me that I am NEVER ALONE.

*****

This past week I began a grief program. I was hesitant to do it, but it has been a pretty powerful experience. One thing I have learned in the past week is that crying is healing. There is no weakness in it, and we shouldn't be apologizing for it. To suppress it is to do us harm, but we have to build that space to do it in. I know that throughout these eight and a half months there have been people who have felt that "Libby is in denial." Well, maybe so. And there is a purpose for that. It is a time where we can determine WHO among family and friends will ALLOW you the ability to mourn ... not grieve but mourn. Grieving is the INTERNAL "stuff". Grief is what happens to us PHYSICALLY when we lose a loved one. Mourning is the EXTERNAL "stuff". For many of us the mourning is the tough stuff. Because our society is uncomfortable with that. We shove it all down because not many want to see it and not many want to hear it. So we have to find that circle of friends and family who WILL allow us to mourn and until then we live in denial.

Ask yourself if you have been that person for someone you know who is grieving. Have you allowed them to MOURN in your presence? It's life changing for that family or friend. It helps us to heal. For those who have ALLOWED me to MOURN with you I thank you with all my heart. Today after our closed conference grief meeting, I paused to do the exercise that was shared with us and suggested that we try. "Sit in a chair, Allow the chair to HOLD you. Try and relax. Focus on your breath." I did.

But I didn't just sit in "a chair." I went into the adjoining room to the main living space of my home. (I just typed that, "my home.") The "sunroom." A room yet unfurnished but for one chair. The chair lovingly referred to by my grandson as "Papa's chair." The chair my husband loved to sit in and did all the time. A recliner. I have not sat in that chair but for a few seconds since he died. My son and my grandson just recently sat in it and my son read a book to my grandson just like Loren would do ... all the time. But I have not been able to sit in that chair. Until today. I allowed that chair to HOLD me. I even put the footrest up and laid back in it. I closed my eyes listening to the Christmas music playing and let the chair HOLD me.

When I opened my eyes the sun was coming through the window and I could hear Loren saying to me, "Look at you resting, being at peace. I know you haven't felt that in the past day or so. I am here. I am with you. Find the joy. You have always LOVED Christmas! YOU were always the BIGGEST kid at Christmas! If you knew there was a present around for you somewhere it wasn't safe! The hot chocolate flowed by the gallons and the cookies were in abundance. It's okay Libby, you are allowed to feel the joy of the season because I AM with you. Every second of every day." I had to go get my camera and take a picture of the beautiful sun shining through the window. It brought me peace, it brought me hope and it refreshed me. So much so that I went in and finished wrapping all my Christmas gifts. Not because I thought I HAD to or NEEDED to, but because I WANTED to. In those moments I was reminded that I am NEVER ALONE.

*****

I cannot swallow right now. About a month before Loren died we were sitting downstairs watching TV together. All of a sudden he looked over at me and said, "You know I don't believe in all that stuff." I asked, "What stuff"? "You know, all that Long Island Medium stuff that you like to watch. But I want you to know that I will find a way to let you know that I am okay." I was dumbfounded by the fact that he had started this conversation with me. I told him that was okay if he didn't believe it, but that I did and I would be open to anything if the time came for me to know. Loren died on April 8, 2015. A week later on a Friday we had his funeral. On Monday I went back to work. We were close to the end of the school year and my plan was to just hold on until then and then go to Ohio and spend time with my family. I did.

When I came back I decided I was going to sell the house and I began the cleaning out and packing up. I have always been quite orderly and not a pack rat. I kept things in the house in order, but the garage was Loren's domain. For years, and I do mean YEARS I would tell him he should purge "his" garage. "Oh no, I might need something." Well, that never happened, and I was left to take care of it. Alone ... but for the help of one of my neighbors who did come down when he saw the two bagsters out on the driveway. In fact, I think I would have had a break down had he not come. That night I sat in my bed, sobbing. I told Loren how hard this was and how I didn't know if I could do this by myself and that I needed to know if he knew how hard this was. I kept asking "Where are you? I need you here. Are you with God? I need to know if you are there with HIM"? The next day I started in the kitchen. Packing and purging. The very last drawer I did was the little desk drawer ... the "junk" drawer as we often referred to it and that everyone has. I continued sobbing throughout the morning.

When I got to the very bottom of this drawer I found this. A card. It is not dated, and I don't even recall when he had given it to me, but it was something he rarely did, he rarely gave me cards, but for special occasions. When I read the words I was reduced to deep sobbing, for how long I don't know. I keep this card by my bedside and read it often to remind me that he IS around me and he DOES hear me.

The "where are you question" was answered when I began cleaning his things out. I found this in his writing on a sticky note inside a book in his nightstand.

Matthew 13:44-46

What could have struck him in such a way that he would write this down?

44 "The kingdom of heaven is like treasure hidden in a field, which a man found and covered up. Then in his joy he goes and sells all that he has and buys that field.

45 Again, the kingdom of heaven is like a merchant in search of fine pearls,

46 who on finding one pearl of great value, went and sold all that he had and bought it".

I no longer have a question as to "where" Loren is or that he knows what I am feeling or what I am doing. He has found his treasure. I am so grateful...and I am NEVER ALONE.

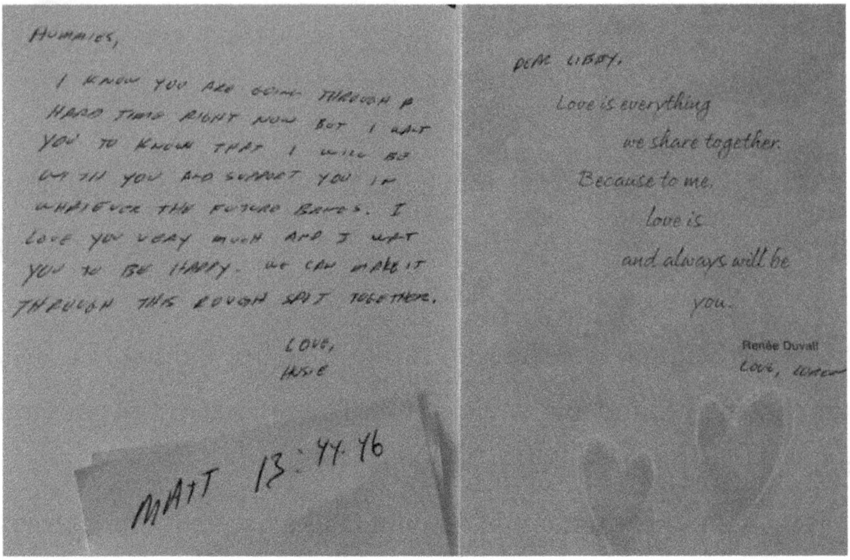
Love is everything
we share together.
Because to me,
love is
and always will be
you.
Renée Duvall
MATT 13:44-46

*****

Today is the second wedding anniversary of our daughter Marie. My heart breaks every time I think of her future without her Dad who she adored. When I look at this picture it is so hard for me to believe that only four months later we received the diagnosis of brain cancer. But today I will rejoice in the memories of this day. I love this photo.

*****

The exercise for today in the grief program I am taking part in suggests "buying a gift from my beloved" to myself. The irony of that is that I would often buy my gifts and then tell Loren he could wrap them up and put them under the tree for me. He rarely could surprise me, but on occasion he did. During this past week I did order two things "from Loren to me" and have written my note as it was also suggested we do:

My Dear Hummies, Merry Christmas!

I wanted you to have these two special pieces of jewelry from your favorite jewelry designer. First of all because for you no special occasion was complete without something from your favorite line of jewelry. But the pieces themselves have special meaning to me for you.

I chose the ring for you because it goes with the enhancer and earrings you bought when you went to West Chester. I was there with you. I was so proud of you. Mostly because you listened to me. You heard my voice calling to you ~ "Look at the flights, Libby." Over and over again I called to you, and I'm so glad you listened and that you went! Yes! You "put your big girl panties on!" And when you arrived you smiled, and you laughed, and you loved every moment that you were there. I was there too. I was watching. And I know you knew I was there because I heard you telling Celeste that you felt me there beside you. When you wear this ring I want you to remember the first time that you traveled to a special event without me beside you and that you CAN enjoy your life!

The second piece is a cuff with floating butterflies. You know they represent "new life". No, they aren't the "Luna", but this is as close as I could get for you. You know I have "new life". I have told you I have "found my treasure"! But YOU have "new life" as well. I see you living it. I know some days are very hard, but most days I see you, like these butterflies, floating above the sadness. You are doing your best to CHOOSE "new life." I see you. I walk beside you. I lay next to you at night while you clutch my cross next to your heart. I hear you asking God and me to give you strength for each day. HE hears you too. HE sees you being obedient to the journey he has put in front of you.

I want you to know how much I love you and how thankful I am to have had you loving me through my illness. I tried to tell you in the end, I hope you knew it.

Wear these beautiful pieces and know when you do I will be smiling because you are choosing "new life."

I love you forever, Loren

*****

Christmas may not be as I had expected it would be. My daughter Marie and her husband Michael had made plans to be here late on Christmas Eve from Oklahoma City, I just received word that Michael's beloved grandfather died this morning. We have been talking the past couple of days about his grandfather's condition worsening and that plans could possibly be changing. To be honest I'm not really sure if anything will or not. But, I think I have prepared myself for them not being here. I do not have a "plan B" and I'm okay with that too. In fact, after nearly 35 years of cooking nearly every Thanksgiving and every Christmas dinner I'm good with just hanging out in my quiet little cocoon. And I am being quite honest about that. However,

I have been busy making some yummy munchies in preparation ... just in case.

*****

I've always loved this time of year ... this time of the day ... when the trees are black silhouettes against the evening sky. Winter Solstice ... so lovely.

*****

I have been listening to Christmas music this morning. Let us be "giving" and "forgiving" to ourselves this Christmas ... so says the line in the song I am listening to. This has been one of my favorite Christmas songs for I don't know how many years. I've been readying packages to ship this morning and this song began to play ..."The trick is to live with love from the start and to give with an open heart"... I want to live with love in my heart, not sorrow ... that is my intention this Christmas.

*****

I love the sound of running water. I always have. My favorite time of the day is my morning bath. It's like a religious experience for me. It's where I "center" myself for the day. Loren always used to laugh at me. He would say, "you are not giving up that long luxurious bath for anything are you?" Nope. In my new home the master bath only has a shower. Which really disappointed me at first. So in the mornings I have to go to the main bathroom to take my bath. I've made peace with that.

But this morning I woke up early and I couldn't go back to sleep. The longer I laid there I thought, "I'm going to get up and I'm going to take a shower". After all the obligatory washing of the hair and body I just stood there under the running water. I stood there and stood there and stood there. No, I wasn't crying ... I was cleansing ... cleansing my heart and my soul and I was breathing ... I don't even know how long I stood there. I think the water conservationists would not be very happy with me. But it is what I needed this morning. It felt so good to just stand there under that running water, listening to it, feeling it. It was most definitely a "religious experience" this morning. It was a really long shower this morning honey ... I am healing ...

*****

Tomorrow would have been Loren's sixtieth birthday. Tonight I am sitting quietly remembering the man I spent more than three quarters of my life with. I can remember so many times watching him walk away from me, into a store, into the gas station, anywhere really, and I would think to myself, "What an amazing man. I am so lucky to be married to a man who takes such good care of himself." I would often tease him how he would be wheeling me around in a wheelchair when I was sixty-five, so he better continue to take good care of himself. I'm smiling at this memory. How I wish we could have celebrated my fifty-fifth birthday together in September. How I wish we could have celebrated our thirty-fifth wedding anniversary together in October and how I wish we could be celebrating his sixtieth birthday together tomorrow.

Instead I will remember the extraordinary man he was, the love he had for me and for his family and that he has the most incredible gift anyone could receive. He has gone "HOME". He has "found his treasure". I will remember this, and I will smile. I am healing ... and I am NEVER ALONE.

*****

It is two days away from Christmas and today would have been Loren's sixtieth birthday. For a moment, my eyes fill with tears at the thought and then I stop and think to myself, "what would my life have been like without this extraordinary man in it?" and "remember what endless joy and peace he is experiencing today and the many gifts he brought to your life and the gifts he left behind." And I stop and think about the person I am becoming because of my experience and my relationship with Loren. A "shift in perception" ... I can feel the miracle happening in my life.

*****

Today is Loren 's birthday, his sixtieth. I imagine it is a day I could have looked towards with "dread". But THAT word was NOT my intention. And so, I feel it has been full of so many precious moments, starting with time with my sister on FaceTime and opening her Christmas gift to me together, and then learning that Marie and Michael will in fact be spending ALL of Christmas with me ... including Christmas dinner! That was not even a thought originally, so I made a mad dash off to the grocery store and Honey Baked Ham so I could be prepared for Christmas dinner.

Then my dear friend Father John came to pick me up for a birthday lunch celebration for Loren. When we finished lunch we came back to my place and we shared the lemon meringue pie that I had baked to celebrate Loren's birthday ... his favorite, and we shared stories from the past twenty plus years. It's wonderful to make new friends, but it is so good to share stories with someone who has known you for years and speaks the name of your beloved without fear of opening the floodgates. Happy doesn't even begin to describe what I feel today!

*****

It is almost 2AM and I cannot sleep. It's as if I am a kid anticipating the arrival of Santa Claus! You remember that feeling, right? I was laying here tossing and turning and thinking about my day yesterday. Loren's birthday which was a day I wasn't really looking forward to ... and now it's in the past. And you know what? I did it! I walked through that day. NO, I LIVED through that day and it was special, and I was HAPPY and so many things throughout the day brought me JOY! And as I laid here in the bed thinking about it all I realized that THAT is what the REST of my life can be like! I don't have to wonder any more "if I can do this" because I DID DO IT!

And while I was thinking about all of that the first time Loren and I visited Ireland in May 2009 popped into my memory. I had waited my entire life to go there, and it had finally come and when I stepped to the wall at the Cliffs of Moher it was the most extraordinary moment! At first I cried and then I was like a kid! It was like the scene at the beginning of the Sound of Music! I could barely contain myself. That's what I feel like RIGHT NOW! If I could do that yesterday than what are the possibilities for the REST of my life!?

Loren will ALWAYS be with me. Our life together, who he was to me and to our family is part of who I am today. Our experience together in the last year of his life has changed me. But what I have experienced in this past eight months, all of it, the pain, the loneliness, the happiness, the joy is what is creating the NEW me. Laying there thinking about it makes me excited. This is the NEW me! This is the feeling I want to remember with each day that comes, each NEW day! And to remember that I am NEVER ALONE.

*****

I have just spent the last two hours with a friend. I met her shortly after I began working at school when her husband had just died suddenly while away on a business trip. I watched her. I watched her live her life. And within a month of knowing her I wrote her a card sharing with her how I felt since I had gotten to know her. Recently I shared with someone how I felt she had been put in my life for a reason, for as we all know, there are no coincidences, "there is no randomness" to our lives. What a morning it was. We laughed and we cried, and we talked about what a blessing our husbands were to our lives.

Time with her was a beautiful gift today. It WILL be a peaceful, joy filled Christmas and I am looking forward to it.

*****

I am feeling lonely this evening ... Marie and Michael won't be here until very late and I am praying for their safe travels as there is flooding all around north Georgia. After spending time with my dear friend and pastor Father John yesterday I was telling him that I was apprehensive about attending Christmas Eve Mass if it meant I would be doing it alone. He said that he "trusted what I needed to do" and that I needed to do whatever it was that my heart felt was the right thing to do.

Marie just texted that they are leaving Chattanooga ... so I have decided I am staying home rather than attending Mass. It will be a very different Christmas for sure, but I'm okay with that. My goal for the next couple of days is to hold on and hold on some more. I can do this. I can live with joy and happiness through this holiday season.

*****

It is my first Christmas without Loren ...

It's 5AM and it's storming again. I can't sleep ... again. Is it Christmas? I don't ever remember a stormy Christmas ... ever. I've been laying here for quite some time. Watching the lightening, listening to the thunder and music quietly playing next to me. I'm trying to figure out how I'm "feeling". I don't have an answer. I don't really "feel" anything. I don't feel sad; I don't feel happy ... I don't feel anything. I wonder if everything will come crashing in on me later.

It has been a beautiful morning of sharing laughter and tears, many tears with my precious Mimi and her husband Michael. I feel so blessed that they have allowed me over and over again throughout the morning and this afternoon to share so much of this journey in the past days with them.

We began the morning by lighting a candle and lifting our glasses (Mimosa's yum) to Loren and "saying his name" and remembering Christmases past. I had to take a picture of the danishes we made for breakfast. They were Loren's favorite Christmas morning tradition. I remember one Christmas a couple of years ago when the whole family was home suggesting to him that we not have the danishes. WHAT? He would just NOT hear of that! So when I went shopping the other day there was just no way we were not going to have danishes with our Christmas morning breakfast. Then we began opening presents. I had to share a photo of Mimi opening her book. She began crying as she read my inscription to her and I shared with her that this book has changed my life, and that I wanted her to read it and reread it and share it with Michael as his precious Grandfather just died this past week. I am so happy that this book, truly a gift, was under the tree for her.

I opened my gift "from my beloved" and read the letter "from him" aloud. We were all crying by the time I finished. When the gifts were finished, I shared with them about the "white envelope" story I had read about this week. I asked Mimi to go to the tree so we could begin our new tradition in Loren's name this Christmas. I am so glad she was here to share in this today. Of course there were more tears. Mourning together ... another gift received this Christmas. Feeling so blessed today. New life in every moment of this first Christmas without Loren physically here, but his presence is EVERYWHERE. And we are NEVER ALONE.

It is later in the morning and it has occurred to me that it is not a "lack" of feelings I am experiencing but that I am experiencing "acceptance". An acceptance that although Loren has left his physical body and gone "home" that he is still beside me. What I imagine I was "feeling" was a feeling of "peace" in the knowledge of that. Although I didn't realize it in that moment. Not until I allowed my thoughts to move towards Loren this morning. Will I have moments of sad emotions today? No doubt. But my intention is not to dwell on them. After all we will celebrate Christ's birth today, the King of Peace! When I think of Loren being in HIS presence it brings me such JOY!!! Merry Christmas everyone!

*****

A letter to my sweetheart ... my first Christmas since you went HOME:

Hello My Honey,

I know that you were so very present with me, with all of us during Christmas. I could feel you throughout the day as Mimi and Michael and I spoke often of you. I was happy because my intention was to finally spend time talking to Mimi about what this journey has been like for the past nine months. We started the morning having your favorite Danishes. I just couldn't see Christmas morning without them. We so enjoyed them, and we toasted to you knowing that you were enjoying the most incredible Christmas gift of all.

After breakfast we opened gifts. Did you like the new tradition for you that I started this year? I'm sure you did. You talked so often about how you wanted to go back to work so that you could "give back" the way we had been given to the entire year of your illness. I want you to know that my plan is to do that as often as I can, in your name. I know you would want me to. I read the letter "from you" when I opened your gift. We all cried and when I finished Mimi said that she could most definitely hear your voice in those words. It was a quiet day and one of much reflection on your life, our life, and my life since you have been gone.

The day after Christmas Matt came with our two little men. Logan is getting so big. I bought him several books and of course one of them was the new "Pete The Cat" book. When he opened it I asked him who loved "Pete The Cat" books? And he said, "Papa". I asked him later in the day if I could read it to him and he immediately got it and sat in my lap. My mind flashes to you and Logan sitting in "Papa's chair" reading together. I choke back tears every time I do. Ollie is such a little guy, but I can only picture him sitting with you on the bed in hospice beside you. He sat next to me on the couch playing with the laptop. Your picture is on the front. I talked to him about you and said, "Say 'hi' to Papa, he loves you so much." He was so cute waving and waving and blowing kisses at your photo. It felt as if you were right there waving back. Really. I think you were. They spent the night, which I wasn't expecting ... sure missed you being here helping. I was so tired. I can't believe it is no longer "Papa and Lala". It is so hard having the boys here and knowing it is no longer "Papa and Lala". It breaks my heart. Every day I remind myself that you are exactly where you are supposed to be and that your only concern for me was to "be okay". So, every day when my feet hit the floor whether it's just an ordinary day, or it was your sixtieth birthday or Christmas day I work hard each day to "be okay". I do, and I will continue to. I hope that I am making you proud. You will forever be a part of me ... who I am and who I will become. I love you.

Your Hummies

*****

"The tragedy of life is not death ... but what we let die inside of us while we live." ~ Norman Cousins

I am sitting here thinking about some of the conversations I had with my friend and her husband tonight. I was sharing with them that something that has brought me the most peace in this journey is that I feel Loren died at the time he did because he had fulfilled all of what God had put him here to do. I know that all death can be considered a "tragedy", but that it would be even MORE of a tragedy to allow myself to die more each day because of Loren's death. I decided that I was going to LIVE my life, because as strange as it seems sometimes I think that Loren died for me. What we experienced throughout the year of his illness and his death was for me to see things within myself that I never knew were there.

I truly feel that this was one of the purposes of Loren's life. God how I hate that he had to go through everything he did and die for that purpose, and I am not egotistical enough to believe that it was his only purpose in life, but I am SO certain it was one of them. How could I NOT LIVE my life with that realization? How it would dishonor his life to realize it and yet still choose NOT to LIVE. I wonder what goes through people's minds when they hear me talk about these things? Do they think "how heartless that her husband is dead not even a year and she is talking about how much she is looking forward to living HER life?", or do they think, "Wow, I hope that I can see my life in the same way when someone I love dies." I wonder ...

*****

I am sitting here this morning reflecting on the fact that this year is coming to an end. I can't help but think how many times Loren would say in the beginning of 2015, "I don't know what happened to 2014, I lost the whole year." A long discussion would follow that comment about how 2015 would be different. It was, and it was not. I now find myself saying the same thing. My prayer for myself and for all of us is that in 2016 we are far more present and that we truly EXPERIENCE life for ourselves and for our loved ones. God bless.

*****

It's pouring rain A-G-A-I-N! And I've been laying here for the past hour trying to make myself get OUT of this bed ... I CAN'T ... and I just leaned over and turned on my music. After Loren died was the first time I had ever heard this piece by composer Kurt Bestor, "The First Morning." I'm not sure why, but when I did it immediately had me sobbing and I have reacted the same way every time I have heard it. Until yesterday. Strangely, as my music played on and off throughout the day this piece probably played three times. Not one tear. Not once. I thought of Loren when I heard it, but I didn't shed a tear. I am healing ... I think ...

*****

Before I went to bed last night, I may have had an "Ah ha" moment about the music. When I went to bed last night, I had a conversation with Loren about showing me a sign of his presence today. I couldn't get out of bed this morning and as I laid there, I thought about how much I loved this time of year when I would be out of school and Loren would take vacation time. Some mornings we would just lay there all curled up. I'd have my legs thrown over his and more times than not he would complain about my feet being cold. It made me smile thinking about those times. Then I leaned over and pressed the button on my iPod and that was the song that came on and after my head was full of thoughts of Loren ... and that I could smile and not cry. Loren was with me and helping me to know that my life is going to be full of so many more moments to remember and smile about than to remember and cry about. I am healing ...

*****

Fear Not.
For I AM with You
I AM YOUR GOD
I will strengthen You
I WILL
help You
I will uphold You
with My righteous
Right Hand
ISAIAH 41:10
jh

Words read and held in our hearts so often during Loren's illness and turned to time again in the nine months since his death. While I do admit being prayerful has been difficult since Loren's death these words will be the words I will carry with me as this year comes to an end and the new year begins. HE is my God, and HE will uphold me and strengthen me ... even when I cannot pray.

*****

It is New Year's Eve and today would have been my parents sixtieth wedding anniversary. Last week would have been Loren's sixtieth birthday. Two of the most important men in my life gone and neither one of them able to celebrate a sixtieth milestone. My heart is full of sadness.

~

January 2016

~

Another fresh new year is here,
Another year to live!
To banish worry, doubt, and fear,
To love and laugh
and give!

- William Arthur Ward

*****

I have spent time this morning reading through my "journal" through 2014 and 2015. I read through the month of December of 2014 realizing that I had not posted for January 1st of 2015, but that New Year's Eve showed the fears, the trials and the exhaustion of so many months before ...

"The end of a year with so many trials and so many tears ... what will the new year bring? Help me Dear Father to know you are always by our side."

I have never forgotten the strength I found in myself through the long journey of Loren's illness and the strength and deep faith I saw in him was what strengthened me. I have been "transformed" by the experiences of these almost two years and my hope and prayer is that through the continual "renewing of my mind", the changing of the way of looking at all that has transpired in my life that the transformation will continue and that it will be good and pleasing to God. One cannot know what plans HE has for you, but I plan to be still, to listen and to be obedient to them.

*****

Oh GOD I'm so lonely tonight! For Loren, for my family, for my LIFE that I had! I can't STOP crying! I HATE this! I HATE it!

*****

Last night I needed to curl up onto someone's lap in a fetal position like a baby and feel someone's arms around me and for that person to allow me to just sob. Sob and rant until I just couldn't anymore. I had no one's arms around me, but for only the third time in the nine months since Loren has died I allowed myself to do that. I don't know if it is as effective doing it that way as opposed to doing it with someone else present. I know it was lonely. I know that I was able to sleep better.

One thing that went through my mind once the tears were spent as I laid there looking out the window was that light always comes after darkness. I will hold that thought in my heart and mind as I begin again today.

*****

"Tearless grief bleeds inwardly" -
Bovee

There was no internal bleeding going on in me last night ... it was a full-on hemorrhage. It feels so much better today!

*****

Today after mass a woman walked up to me and said, "You made it through the holidays." She had tears in her eyes as she said it. I didn't want to be rude and correct her. What I wanted to say was, "No, no I didn't "make it through", I "LIVED" through the holidays. It was a choice.

Several months after Loren died I found myself saying, "I won't be DOING the holidays this year. No tree, no decorations, no baking, nothing." That didn't last long. As I immersed myself into learning a different way to do grief I realized that the biggest sadness would be not honoring Loren and what he would want me to do. He would most definitely want me to celebrate the holidays. It wasn't always easy. But I found many moments of joy, happiness and celebration of Loren. In early Fall I remember thinking of these few months with dread. The anticipation of my fifty-fifth birthday, our thirty-fifth wedding anniversary, Thanksgiving, Loren's sixtieth birthday, Christmas and the New Year. So much in such a short period of time. I honestly didn't know if I could "do it". But I did. The anticipation of all those things was far worse than the actual day. Was it all different? Yes. Was it lonely? At times. Was there sorrow and sadness? Again, at times. Was it worth "living through" it all? A most definite yes. I learned it can be done and I can do it with the knowledge that there should be no guilt about wanting to LIVE my life. What matters most is LIVING my life which begins again with each new day. Light follows darkness always ... and I am NEVER ALONE.

*****

Sigh ... I had music playing all day today as I was packing the Christmas decorations up. But I would go from one thing to the other. Never accomplishing a whole heck of a lot. So many songs played today that brought so many memories flooding back. I tried not to let them make me sad. “Reminiscing” this song was one of “our songs"... and here come the tears. But they were short lived and just kind of wistful and not full-on heart wrenching. I am healing.

*****

"Be Joyful in Hope, Patient in Affliction, Faithful in Prayer"
Romans 12:12

I was awake early this morning and spent a lot of time in thought and prayer about Loren's death nine months ago tomorrow.

This morning my prayer was assisted by my devotional as I read through both todays and tomorrow's devotion. Tomorrow. Tomorrow is 9 months since Loren went HOME. Yes, he did. He went HOME to our Heavenly Father. And while his physical presence in my life is something I long for it brings me such peace to have the knowledge of where he is and that I had the privilege of watching him prepare himself for that not only during the year that he was ill, but throughout our life together.

Throughout Loren's illness and in these past 9 months, admittedly I have not always found it easy to pray. But I have remained faithful in my hope in HIM. HIS promise to all of us, that like Loren we will go HOME to HIM when we have completed all that we have come here to do. I will remain "joyful in hope" at that knowledge. Yes, I will. And I will do my best to remember that I am NEVER ALONE.

*****

Today the wind has been relentless, especially through this afternoon. It is literally howling through the attic space of this place, and I couldn't help thinking how sorrowful it sounded. After hours of listening to it I couldn't take it. So I went where I have been going when I feel like this. My shower. I figured the sound of the water would drown out the howl of the wind. I turned the hot water on as hot as I could stand it and stood there for more than a half an hour. Sobbing ... sobbing, but strangely there were no tears. Is that what happens when you are angry grieving? Because I was. And for the first time I think I was angry at Loren. In almost ten months I don't think I have been angry AT Loren. But today I was.

It started with me thinking as I stood there under the running water with this thought. "Loren would hate that I am wasting water just standing here with it running." At first I thought I should turn it off, but then I started feeling pissed. I thought to myself, "To damn bad." Then I thought, "To damn bad because I HATE a lot of things! I HATE that YOU DIED! I HATE that you had BRAIN CANCER! I HATE that I watched you become so weak and not able to do ANYTHING, even walk! I HATE that we PRAYED and PRAYED and PRAYED and you STILL DIED! I HATE that everyone smiles at me and says "we have to get together “and then they NEVER call! I HATE that I am fifty-five years old, and you LEFT ME!"... you get the picture.

The rants kept coming and the sobs with no tears. In the past few weeks I have noticed lines that have shown up on my face that weren't there. These aren't "normal" lines. These are lines that speak of sorrow and pain. They weren't there and now they are. These aren't the lines I want. I want lines that speak of joy and happiness. Not lines that when someone looks at my face they can see something else carried inside. For the first time I am angry at him. He doesn't deserve that. He doesn't, and I don't know how to stop feeling the anger right now.

*****

Nearly every morning since Loren died I take the time to breathe and to listen to this beautiful piece by composer Paul Cardall. “Redeemer”. I am reminded that HE walked with us through the valley. That HE was there waiting for Loren and that HE continues to walk with me throughout each day. BREATHE...

*****

Sometimes I wander through this world wondering if anyone ever takes notice, really takes notice. Today while I was out and about I was checking out in a store and the woman behind the counter asked me if I worked at Piedmont Fayette Hospital. I told her no, but that I had spent a lot of time there. She nodded her head and said that I looked familiar to her because she was a volunteer there. She asked me if I had been sick and I told her no, but my husband had been. Of course she then asked me if he was doing better ... I smiled and said, "Yes, yes he is doing better." I told her he had died nine months ago. At first I think she was rather surprised by my response. She continued to check me out quietly. I think she was trying to decide how to respond to what I had told her. As she handed me my bag she said, "I am truly sorry for your loss." I thanked her and then I thanked her for remembering me. I guess sometimes people do stop and take notice.

*****

There was a time, only months ago when I would listen to this song by composer Kurt Bestor, "The First Morning", and I would fall apart. Deep, deep sorrow would overcome me. I'm not sure why. It just touched something within me.

Recently when I have listened to it instead of crying I sit quietly and just experience the beauty of it. I reflect and I pray, and I realize I am healing. What once brought me such pain now allows me to be prayerful. So, like one of the little friends in our class will often say, "Oh help me Jesus!" Help me heal, help me find joy, help me find peace, and today help me to know that I am NEVER ALONE.

*****

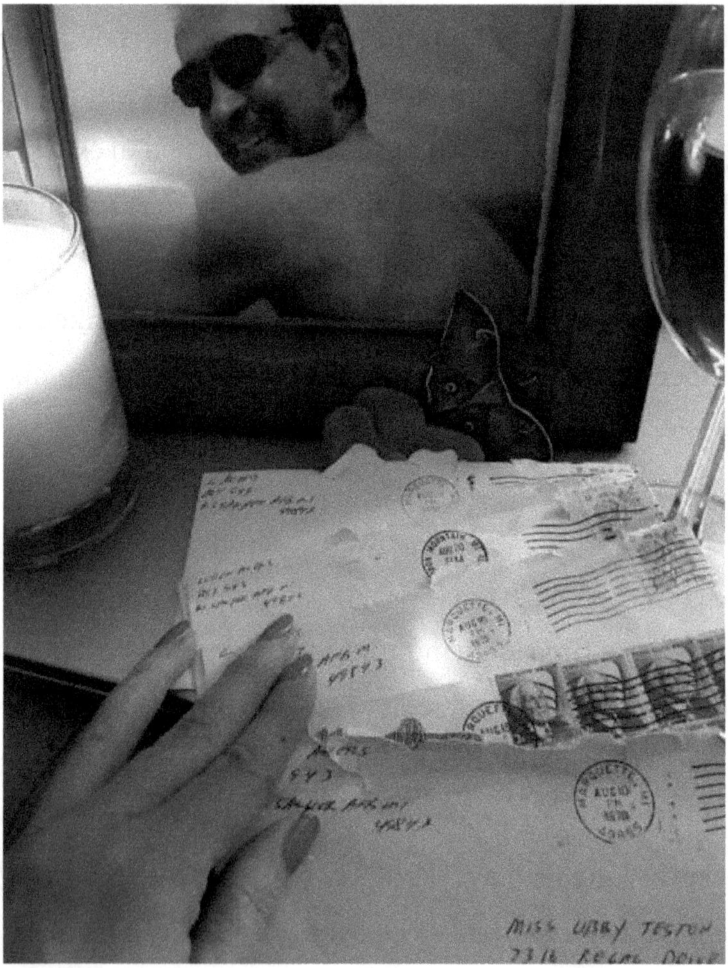

I've been spending time tonight doing something that I've been wanting to do since I found the box while getting ready to move to my new home. Letters from Loren that he began writing just days after returning back home after meeting him when he came for my brother's wedding in August of 1978. I wasn't ready before, but something made me pull the box down from the closet tonight. I thought I would cry but I haven't shed a tear. I have smiled non-stop remembering the sweetness of that time. The happiness, the excitement and joy of this new love. I can't wait to continue reading through these letters that tell our story ... at least the beginning of it, and I am so happy that I saved them. All of them. I am healing...

*****

For some reason today my thoughts have raced from remembering "the beginning" to remembering "the end". Although not really "the end" because we are forever in relationship with those we love who have gone HOME. Maybe it has been the mindless activity of ironing panel after panel of curtains and listening to beautiful instrumental music. Many songs from "the beginning". HOPE has been my "theme" of the day. Healing takes work, very hard work every day. Today I have been staying focused on being hopeful for what lies ahead for me. What is the path that HE has for me? I'm not certain but I went and paged through my journal that I was encouraged by Loren's doctor, Dr. Dunbar to write. I am happy I did that.

Although sometimes it is painful to go back though the journey of Loren's illness, I am also reminded of Loren's strength and the faith that kept him always hopeful. It also reminds me of my own strength and that I am truly NEVER ALONE.

*****

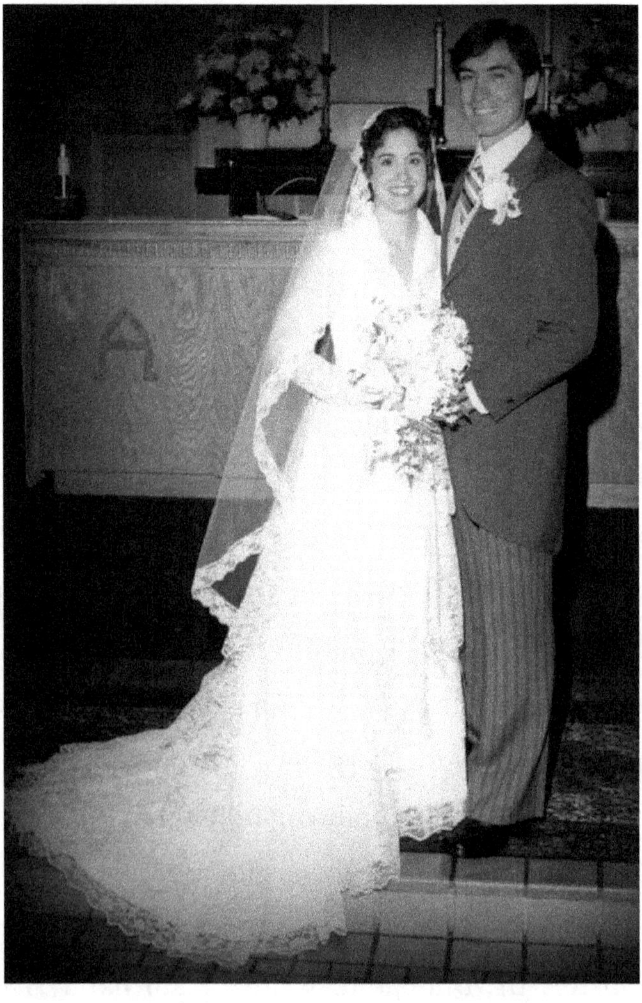

In all the years we were married it never mattered to him that I didn't stay the little ninety-eight-pound waif in this picture, that after four kids and hypothyroidism there have been times that I weighed as much as he did. It didn't matter. He always told me I was beautiful and that I mattered more than anything else in the world. That's who he was. As beautiful on the inside as he was on the outside. How blessed I am that he spent the rest of his life with me. The other picture? One of his favorite past times with my brothers. You could always hear the sound of those weights clinking away down in the basement. Annoying ... but he looked damn good doing it!

*****

So this morning I am having an omelet for breakfast for the first time in probably at least a year. Big deal, right? Don't lie I can hear you thinking it! Well I can tell you it IS a big deal. Loren LOVED to make breakfast. Most especially he loved to make ME breakfast. I can hear his voice right now, "Hummies, Whatcha want me to fix you for breakfast?" My answer? An omelet. Always an omelet. He was a really good omelet maker. I have missed those times. Lazy Saturday mornings and Sundays after church. This morning I decided to eat an omelet. Not eating one was really not something I did consciously, at least I don't think so. Maybe I'm wrong. Again, think it's no big deal? When someone you love dies your mind, your body and your heart do things that you might never imagine.

*****

Today is feeling like one of those days that the best I will be able to do is to hold on ... some days are like that ... and it's okay ... a day I am having a hard time remembering that I am NEVER ALONE.

*****

Social media ... can't live with it ... can't live without it. Today a memory from one year ago showed up. It was a photo that I had taken of a beautiful sunrise from the window of the hospital room we were in as Loren was there with severe symptoms of his cancer. In fact we had learned that the cancer had metastasized to his spine. In just over two months he died.

It has been almost an entire year since his passing. Sometimes it feels as if I am living someone else's life, or having an out of body experience ...

*****

"Faith isn't a feeling it is a choice"

I have read this quote many times in the past year and a half.

Yesterday I had a long overdue conversation with my sister. While she is seven years younger than me, often times she is much wiser and if you can believe this, you who have known me for a long time, she can be far more outspoken than me. Yesterday she asked me a few pointed questions out of concern for me which I answered, and it gave us the opportunity to talk about many things.

I told her how difficult a week it has been as I had been seeing many "memories" on social media that have brought back to me the difficulties of this time last year. A time where it became too hard to deny any longer the reality of what was happening to Loren. And when it began to happen it happened rapidly. She made a comment to me about "faith" and I shared with her a post that I made in the closed grief program that I had joined. I shared with her the pain and the anguish that has been part of me for the past week. It's funny when you feel you have made such "progress" in your grief journey, if there is such a thing, but then you feel as if you are "right back there" again. Back at the beginning of the journey.

Although I must admit that there are so many feelings I have not even dealt with up until now. One of those feelings being anger. And while it seems ridiculous to be angry AT Loren, I have been. A feeling I pray will not last long because frankly, he doesn't deserve my anger, and yet it is there. After I shared these thoughts with my sister, she said to me, "Lib, you are a different person in all of this. You are not the same and I am so proud of you and I know Loren feels the same. Your faith has been there through it all even though you both prayed and prayed for healing and yet still Loren died. And the same with Dad."

I know a huge part of my faith journey was watching Loren and his continued faithfulness to God. I was inspired to continue believing that HE was walking beside us and that HE would direct our path, and my path regardless of the outcome. I have thought of my conversation with my sister so much since yesterday and although we are far apart in age and in miles from one another she has been my biggest support and strength throughout Loren's illness and since his death. So grateful and thankful that she is part of my life. As she always reminds me, "God is good"... and I am NEVER ALONE.

*****

Today I decided that I was sick and tired of feeling sick and tired and lonely on the weekends. In just two months it will be a whole year since Loren has been gone and it was an entire year that he was ill, and several months of him not feeling well before his diagnosis. I am so tired of feeling like I'm not living my life.

So I did something pretty much out of my comfort zone. I got in the car and drove to unfamiliar territory (for me) an hour away to Callaway Gardens. There was an art show going on at the botanical gardens and a lovely lady who creates the most beautiful pottery pieces that I discovered at a craft fair a couple of weeks after Loren died was there. I fell in love with her work, and I have enjoyed the pieces that I purchased that day from her.

Although it was a day alone again it was a beautiful day and a beautiful drive ... breathe.

*****

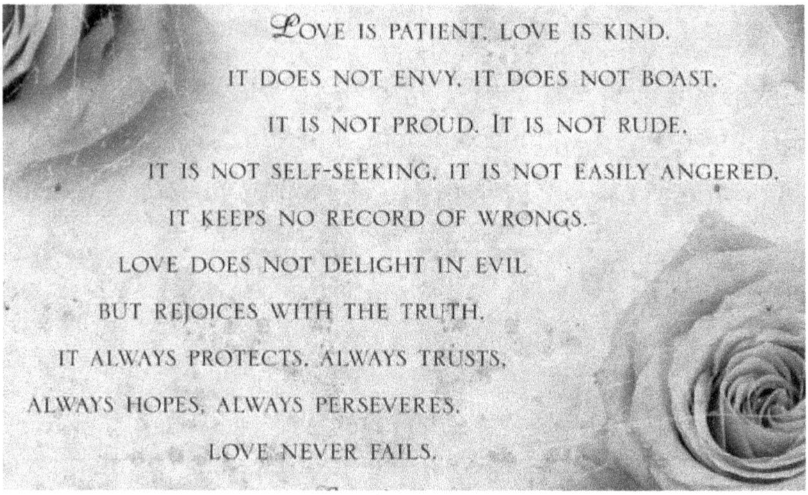
LOVE IS PATIENT. LOVE IS KIND.
IT DOES NOT ENVY. IT DOES NOT BOAST.
IT IS NOT PROUD. IT IS NOT RUDE.
IT IS NOT SELF-SEEKING. IT IS NOT EASILY ANGERED.
IT KEEPS NO RECORD OF WRONGS.
LOVE DOES NOT DELIGHT IN EVIL
BUT REJOICES WITH THE TRUTH.
IT ALWAYS PROTECTS. ALWAYS TRUSTS.
ALWAYS HOPES. ALWAYS PERSEVERES.
LOVE NEVER FAILS.

Grief ...

You try to know in your heart and mind that although you love and miss your loved one so much THEY would want you to, and YOU want to LIVE your life with everything you have within you. But every memory brings with it a tidal wave of others and then you begin to question yourself.

That's what was happening to me this morning before I headed out on my little adventure. While I was getting ready I had memories of those last weeks with Loren. One memory led to another and then another. Memories that began to bring a sadness and heaviness of heart. I have often referred to times like this as post-traumatic stress, because to have these memories brings such sorrow. While feeling this way this morning for some reason these verses from Corinthians came to my mind. We have all heard them time and again. Most often during a wedding ceremony.

As I have so many times before when I have heard them I asked myself the same questions this morning. Was I patient enough? Was my love kind enough? Was I slow to anger? Did my love for Loren protect him enough? Did I always have hope? Did my love persevere for him? Most of all, did I fail him? WAS MY LOVE ENOUGH for all that Loren was going through? I don't know. I don't know the answer to those questions. So, how do you choose to be happy, to find joy in each day, to live your life without knowing if what you did was enough for someone you "say" you loved?

Grief ... sorrow, pain and questions. Always questions.

~

February 2016

~

"And the Lord, He is the One who goes before you. He will be with you; He will not leave you nor forsake you; do not fear nor be dismayed."

Deuteronomy 31:8

*****

February 1st, and I'm just days away from yet another "1st". Another "special occasion" without him.

If you haven't been here then most likely you won't "get it". Honestly, I think this occasion may be one of the hardest for me. I'm sure there will be many flower arrangements being delivered to the workplace and many floral trucks passed on the road as I drive here and there on Valentine's Day.

I will tell you it is hard to be out and about and seeing couples our age and older walking hand in hand and laughing and enjoying conversations with one another the way Loren and I used to. The "1st's" keep coming ... it makes you want to stop the world from spinning and jump off.

*****

One of the hardest things emotionally for me since Loren's death is spending time with my grandchildren. For as long as I can remember Loren talked about being a grandfather and it brought him so much joy when our children began having children.

At the time of his death our grandson Ollie was only six months old. One of my most vivid memories of Loren's illness was when several of our children and our two grandsons came to the hospice to visit with Loren. I have a photo of them gathered around Loren's bed and Ollie is sitting there, Loren's hand around him.

I have several photos of Loren around my new home and each time the grandchildren have come Ollie will look at the photos, wave and say "hi" to his Papa.

I had just put this photo of the two of us out right before they came to visit. Ollie walked over to the photo and as if I were not even in the photo reached out to touch Loren's face and repeated over and over again, "Hi Papa, hi, hi, hi." My son and I just stood there and watched. Be still my heart ... and we are NEVER ALONE.

*****

Yesterday afternoon a co-worker walked up to me with an email that her husband gave to her from one of the managers out at Delta Air Lines. The email had been sent out to the departments in the Technical Operations Center inviting everyone to a fundraiser for Relay for Life in Loren's name. I was so very touched that they also were anticipating the one-year anniversary of Loren's passing and doing this in his honor as Loren would often say that "no one would remember him" when he was gone.

Throughout my visit to the TOC Loren's presence was extremely strong with me. I was overwhelmed with emotion and gratitude for his "family" at Delta Air Lines for proving that he was so wrong. His physical presence is no longer with them, but he is certainly not forgotten.

Proof that Loren was right by my side? The Delta banner sent to the military in 2009 was signed by hundreds of Delta's employees. I had never seen it before but while I stood reading a certificate on the wall next to the banner I wondered to myself if Loren had signed it. I stepped in front of it and in seconds, literally seconds, his name popped up in front of me. Even his friend John was flabbergasted at how quickly I found his name. He is always here. By the way ... this is the best Valentine's Day gift I could possibly have received!

*****

The end of the day has brought me yet another gift. My nephew Alex who is an incredibly talented welder has been making decorative items recently. When I saw the roses he was making I asked him if he thought he could make a pink one for me. Pink roses hold a very special meaning for me. A short time later I received a message from my sister who shared that there was something special on the way. LOVE! A pink rose to treasure forever!

*****

Grief can sometimes make us become very self-centered I have found. I have learned that it is okay to allow myself to be that way. I cannot and will not be able to give to others until I have moved further into my own healing. Healing will be a forever thing, but in time I will be healed enough to be able to give to others once again.

Today Mimi called in on Skype to share with me my valentine gift which she shared had just arrived ... and that she loved it so much she had also gotten one for herself. I am so proud of her. Yes, my husband died. But her Dad did too. A dad who she adored and was the world to her. She has been doing the hard work of healing. We have talked many times of "choosing joy each day". It is hard, hard work to do that. She has gifted us both a reminder ..."Today I Choose Joy". Beautiful! I can't wait until mine arrives!

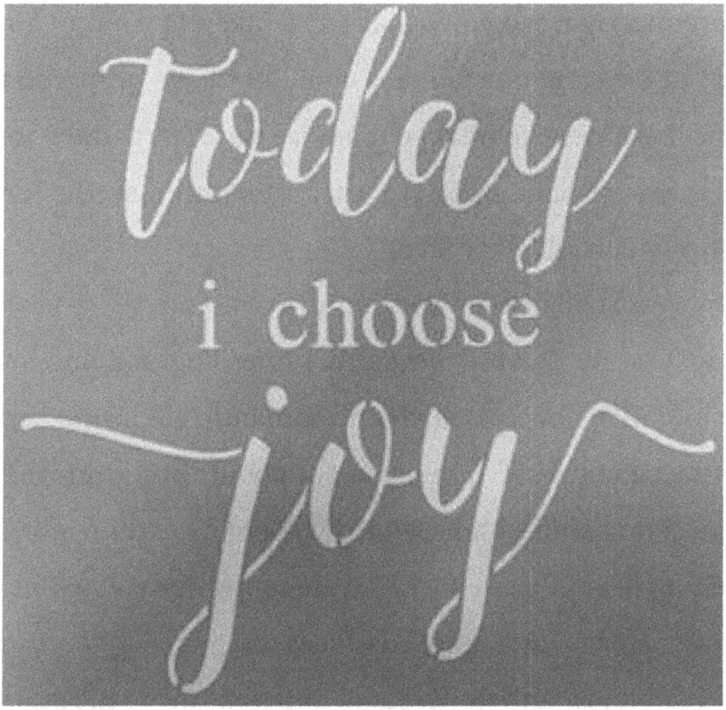

*****

Tomorrow I will experience yet another 1st in my life. My life has been full of "firsts" for far more than the ten months since Loren died.

I am laying here tonight and my memories are full of the "first" time I heard the words "there is a mass on your husband's brain." We were to find out later the full horror of that statement. But those words were the beginning of the "firsts" for me. Honestly, I perhaps was realizing for the "first" time in thirty-four years of marriage what "LOVE" truly means. That the day we were married, the vows that were taken in front of an altar, in front of God and our families could not have prepared us for the words we were to hear so many years later, and the love we would have to call upon to carry us through the darkest challenge we would ever face.

Tomorrow will be the "first" time in over thirty-five years that there will be no flowers, no cards professing undying love, no frilly box full of chocolates and no romantic gift. But I live with the knowledge that love really is not about those "things." Love is about being able to hold your husband's head in your hands and telling him, "I'm so sorry for being so difficult, so mean to you", because his undiagnosed illness was making him someone you did not know and understand and him saying in return, “It's okay honey, you didn't know."

It's about spending night after night for months on end on a pull-out chair in a hospital room so that you are sure the love of your life knows you are there beside him while he fights with every ounce of his being for YOU.

It's about loving someone so deeply that even when you think you have nothing else to give you dig down even deeper because you know he would do that for you ... and he did.

It's about fearing that the time is coming that you have to say goodbye and even though every part of you wants to scream "stay with me", instead you say, "It's okay for you to go". THAT is "love".

Yes, I miss the "I love you's", the flowers, and the gifts, but most of all I miss knowing that the person who loved me most in the world is no longer here to share all of those "things" with. Give not just the "things" tomorrow. Give of yourself, your absolute self.

We have this moment. We never know about the next.

*****

This past week I received some very good advice, from someone who doesn't even know me. He said, "Don't spend time on what is not. Concentrate on what IS and the rest will all take care of itself." So today I will do my best to not waste time on "what is not" and concentrate on "what is".

"What is" is that I am here and as my daughter's gift reminds me, "I Choose Joy"...Today I "choose joy." I will busy myself doing lots of the things that I enjoy doing. Not to forget, but because I believe with all my heart that Loren WANTS me to do these things ... and many, many others. "Concentrating on what IS"... and doing my best to remember that I am NEVER ALONE.

*****

There is an interesting thing that happens when you spend a lot of time alone. You begin spending a lot of time reflecting on the "why" of your life.

I find there is not one definitive answer. I would imagine it is that way for many of us, and we may never really know the answer. We have all heard that there is a "purpose" to each of our lives. I think about that a lot. Especially about Loren's life, because we have also heard that if we believe in God, or whatever you may call "a higher power" that we have been put here with a purpose and that when we complete that purpose we "go HOME".

I'm not certain what I believe about that any longer, or if there is such a thing as ones "purpose" but I know I believe in God. I know that through Loren's illness, the experiences we had together and in this time since his death that our lives together and my life since has been through many transformations.

I have been transformed. I can truly say that I am NOT the person I was nearly two years ago. How could I be? God planned it that way, of that I'm certain. When Loren returned HOME to HIM he also was not the same person he had been the year before. I watched him transform right in front of me. I couldn't imagine him being any more beautiful a human being than he was, but in the end he most certainly was. God's glorious LIGHT had transformed both of us. We had become LIGHT to one another and I pray we had become a LIGHT unto this world through our experience.

I pray that this is the truth ... and that I am learning to be an even brighter LIGHT to the world. Through the grief it is hard some days to SEE "the light", never mind BE "the light", but I pray that through my experiences with each of you, through time shared with you at work, at play or in prayer that somehow I am LIGHT to you and we can be that for one another.

*****

Most days I feel that I am doing an okay job walking along this journey called grief. In fact I recently had someone say to me, "You are 'doing grief' like no one else I know." I'm not sure exactly what that means or if it is even true. But, when I sit in a restaurant by myself and see couples ... older couples than Loren and I are, I can't help but be sad, even angry. This too shall pass, this too shall pass ... and I do my best to remember that I am NEVER ALONE.

*****

It is strange how something can set your emotions reeling. You want to do something because it was something that Loren loved so much but you know it may bring up so many memories that may bring with them the sadness and tears.

Loren always enjoyed having popcorn when he was watching his favorite show, Survivor. In half an hour the season premier of Survivor will start. He never missed a show, in fact last week one of his friends out at Delta was sharing with me how much they enjoyed rehashing every episode. I would sit through the last fifteen minutes of every show while he would analyze every conversation and try to figure out who would get voted off. I would finally look at him and say, "Honey why don't you just wait and see!"

Maybe if I listen hard enough I will be able to hear him trying to figure it all out.

*****

When you are walking this journey of grief there are so many things to try to understand. What I know is that I have had this conversation of "understanding" with 40, 50, 60 and 70 year olds. We all ask the same questions and it doesn't matter how old we are, we are ALL trying to "understand" AND we are ALL aware of the ways "it" (grief) has helped us to grow. If I could have passed on this journey I certainly would have, but God evidently has much more for me to learn and far more for me to figure out.

*****

This morning I had someone who is so dear to me, especially since he spent so much time with Loren during his illness, say something to me that both touched me but also has made me feel ... okay I can't find the right word ... I know right? For someone who can be quite "wordy" that's a change.

He said, "there's still a bit of Shirley Temple in you. That little girl who needs to be taken care of." Like I said, I was touched but at the same time I have spent the better part of these last two years realizing for the first time in my life that I am far more capable of taking care of myself than I EVER thought I could be. I think I will not over think this and just be thankful that there is someone in this world who cares in a sweet way for me, the way Loren did for me ... to be safe, and to be happy. Too much time on my hands ... way too much thinking ... and being way too philosophical.

*****

"Bittersweet" ... that word so often comes to my mind about experiences in my life since Loren died nearly eleven months ago. There are some who would argue that to use this word as it pertains to your life of loss of a loved one is negative. I believe it is a "tender" word. One that describes the love and tenderness of your life journey and memories of your loved one.

I took a whirlwind trip out of town to participate in a retreat for those who are grieving this weekend and doing so brings that word "bittersweet" front and center again. But the experience was not what I think most people would expect. Yes, there were tears for without tears we cannot get the grief "up and out". Without the sacred cleansing tears, we will not find the hope, the joy, the peace that we are longing for.

Sitting on the airplane ... the Delta airplane both going to the retreat and coming home ... the "Home he built for me" my mind was full of love and gratitude to Loren for the thirty-three years of commitment to Delta Air Lines ... and for the thirty-four years of commitment to me and his family and all that he left behind for me. I have not enjoyed the privilege of taking a trip on Delta Air Lines a lot since his death, but when I have it has not been lost on me how amazing our life was because of what he chose to do and how mine has been.

It has not been lost on me how I could sit around and lament about "WHAT IS NOT", but instead I spend my time (most of the time) on "WHAT IS". "WHAT IS" is the beautiful home that I now have because of Loren's love and commitment to what he chose to do in his life and to me and our family. "WHAT IS" is my faith that helps me to know that I can count on strength for the journey from HIM. "WHAT IS" is that with each new day I have a choice ... to live with a heart of gratitude and joy and the knowing that my life, because of the thirty-four years I had with Loren, has been blessed beyond measure and that Loren is always with me. ALWAYS ... I am NEVER ALONE.

*****

I can't even begin to describe the contradiction I feel in my heart, my soul, and my body this week. In conversations I have had with people since returning from a long weekend away attending a retreat the best I can describe it, and as I have also said, I have no point of reference, I feel as if I am coming down off a high on drugs ... at least that is what I imagine it to feel like.

Returning home to an empty place and the beginning of a week of many important responsibilities I was reminded once again of the reality of my life without Loren in it. It has been like a literal slap in the face. Once again I have been filled with what at times feels like overwhelming grief. My mind has been racing with memories of those last weeks with Loren and all of the emotions of that time and honestly the past couple of days have been almost as exhausting as I remember those days to have been.

I sit here looking at the date and I am struggling to remember if this was the day of Loren's final full brain radiation. I think it was. I can't make myself look for those photos because seeing them reminds me of how Loren did not even look like himself and I have not wanted to remember him that way. But over and over in the past couple of days I have revisited those days and weeks. I can hardly believe that in just over a month it will be one year since his death ... and yet it feels like it was only weeks ago ... this is where the contradictions begin. And sometimes, as I have shared before, it almost feels as if I have been living someone else's life. Seriously. How could my handsome, healthy, happy husband possibly be gone? How? I could not have possibly spent the past two years of my life in the way that I have. No.

But every morning, every single morning is a reminder ... every morning when my alarm wakes me it takes only a few minutes before the reality of "WHAT IS" sinks in. When I turn to his side of the bed... because I still don't sleep there...to realize that he is not there...and hasn't been...for a year...almost. My feet touch the floor and I walk to the bathroom and realize that he hasn't been there. I can't smell his aftershave and the fact that he had been in the tub and left for work ... like the many years that we had followed one another in that way. I drive to work ... in silence ... no morning phone call ..."Hi honey, how's your morning? What does it look like outside today? (It was always dark when he left for work) Have a good morning, I'll talk to you at lunch". And we did ... nearly every day. I return "home" from work each day ... to silence ... no smell of coffee brewing as I walk through the door. For the longest time I couldn't bring myself "to do" that afternoon ritual. We would share that cup of coffee and talk about our day.

And at night I pull down the bed ... alone ... climb in, and hope that I fall asleep and stay asleep so that I won't be reminded if I do wake that he is not there ...

Almost an entire year ... It seems like yesterday ... some days it seems like forever ... the sad days are not often, but when they are it can be hard to "anticipate feeling joy again." I know I will because I have spent much of the past year "choosing joy"... but some days are hard, some days are very hard ... and I am doing my best to remember that I am NEVER ALONE.

*****

"The Lord is kind and merciful"
Psalm 103:8

Mass tonight ... it has been a few weeks since I have attended. Going to mass has probably been one of the more difficult things for me to do since Loren's death. St. Philips became our "home" from the very first day our feet hit the soil in the state of Georgia. Literally. We checked into our hotel on a Saturday afternoon in May of 1981 and picked up the phone book to find the nearest church. We found St. Philips and attended mass that evening. It was the place we raised our family, where they received their sacraments and where our faith life was nurtured and grew. It is where we found our strength in the year of Loren's illness and where so many people supported and loved us through that journey. For me now, it is also a place of sadness and loneliness. I look around and see so many of the people we have known for years, the many couples ... some who were so important in our lives as families.

Tonight as I left, yes lonely and a bit sad I turned my thoughts to these words, "The Lord is kind and merciful"... "God is good to all creation, full of compassion", and I began to think of HIS mercy towards me rather than dwell on the loneliness and sadness. I began to think of my "family" at St. Philips and what their love and kindness meant to the both of us through that year. I began to think of Father John and how happy I was that he had come back "home" to St. Philips after being away for a number of years and how fortunate Loren and I were to have him by our side throughout our journey, and how he has continued to love and support me since Loren's death.

"The Lord is kind and merciful"... I have been asked numerous times since Loren died if I am angry, or was I? I was reminded by Father John recently about a night soon after Loren's diagnosis. Father John came up to the hospital in Atlanta. Loren fell asleep and we walked down the hallway together to a little sitting area. He asked, "Do you remember how angry you were?

Do you remember the things you said?" I did and I do. I think it was one of the last times I was THAT angry. And yes, I was angry at God. In fact, I remember laying out some ultimatums to HIM. How silly of me to question God and the path that HE had laid out in front of us.

Tonight I am thankful for HIS mercy and kindness. I am quite certain he expected my anger, and I am so thankful HE sent his loving servant Father John to be by my side for that rant that evening. I am thankful that Loren CHOSE me. He CHOSE me to live the rest of his life with. What an amazing gift! AMAZING! He is now with our Father who is so "kind and merciful", and I am NEVER ALONE.

*****

Over the weekend I spent time reading through the journal I kept almost daily during the year Loren was ill. Sometimes while reading it was as if I was having an "out of body" experience. It was as if I was reading about someone else's life. No. The reality is that it was my life. It was Loren's life. And the reality now is that life all too often for me is lonely and dark.

Over a week ago I went to a retreat and I have mentioned to many people that although the experience was amazing it has been quite difficult reentering the reality of my life. As the days have gone by in this past week I have felt lonelier and in a dark place. I have prayed relentlessly to God to lift me out of the darkness back into the light and hopefulness that I had been feeling. I have asked HIM to help me know and understand what HIS purpose is for me. I have asked for a concrete message to carry with me each day. Help me to know that I am a light for others.

Today HE gave me that concrete answer. After work I had to make a few stops. Before I picked up some groceries I stopped into a store and met up with a sweet lady I have known for years. She walked up to me with tears in her eyes and she shared a very personal story with me about what is happening in her life. What she said to me afterwards will stay with me for a long time. She said, "Libby all I could think of was you and everything that you and Loren went through while he was sick and everything you have been through since. You walked through that with such grace and dignity, and it got me through those days, and I know that I can do this because I have seen you go through one of life's most difficult experiences." Dear God! I asked, and you answered me. Maybe it is not my "life's purpose", but what I have experienced has brought hope and light to someone else's life.

I needed to hear that. I thanked her for sharing her story and I thank God for putting me in that place today. There are no coincidences ... "there is no randomness" ...

I know the darkness and loneliness I have been feeling will pass. God sent me a clear message today of what HE needs me to be. It was a lovely and uplifting experience that I needed to have. And then I walked into my beautiful light filled home and was reminded once again that although the life I am living is not what I would choose I am so blessed ... yes, blessed.

~

March

2016

~

*****

Life is full of uncertainty. My life for the past two years has been full of blatant uncertainty. Two years and I cannot say that I have become comfortable with that. But I am open to the infinite possibilities I may experience if I allow myself to become comfortable with the uncertainty. I will continue to allow myself to feel EVERYTHING I need to feel to continue to heal and to be okay with the uncertainty. My faith tells me that I am NEVER ALONE ... that is the ONE thing I am certain of. Everything else I will remain open to.

*****

"Unworthiness" ... God does not feel we are unworthy, why should we? We attach ourselves to so many words that we shouldn't. This is a word that so many attach themselves to. It is not one I want to attach myself to. Nope, I'm not going there. I have experienced too much in the past two years to allow myself to feel "unworthy" of God's love. In fact, BECAUSE of these experiences I KNOW I am worthy of HIS love for me ...

*****

I am grateful in ALL things and at ALL times. One month from today it will be one year since Loren took his last breath here and breathed his first as he returned to the presence of our creator. One entire year. It doesn't seem possible that an entire year has passed and at the same time it seems as though it was only yesterday.

Throughout his illness we both learned so much about ourselves and about each other. No, neither of us would have chosen to walk that journey. I know I would not have chosen this experience, but through it all I have remained grateful for the love of God and of Loren, for without them I would not have the ability to walk through each day. I choose to continue to heal. I continue to choose to do the hard work each day. I look forward to the day when I feel at peace and a joy that I have not felt for the past two years of my life.

*****

I wish I had recorded the talk that was given at the Lenten mission this evening at church. Frankly, I couldn't even begin to do it justice. It was talked about how important music is to our lives and while I listened my own love for music began to make sense to me.

Music has always been very important in my life. Ironically, I cannot read or play a note, but for as long as I can remember I have listened to it nearly every day of my life. My parents enjoyed music and I remember music often playing in our home.

When I was old enough to buy my own stereo and music I was always listening to it. I would retreat to my bedroom every afternoon when I would get home from school and listen to music for hours. The first week that Loren and I were married we had a conversation about me having music on all the time. He surrendered to the fact that music was a given in our household. Music has never been more important in my life than it has in the past two years. It brought much peace to me and to Loren during his illness. Often we would lay in bed at night, praying as we listened to the beauty of instrumental music. To say that music has been my salvation in this past year is not an understatement. It has been a constant. I wake to it; I prepare myself for my day listening to it. If I could listen to it throughout my day at work I would. When I return home from work I immediately turn my music on, and I go to sleep at night listening to it. It brings me comfort in the loneliness, and in the sorrow. In fact, it often brings the grief up and out.

Music has been my healer. It is where I feel closest to God and closest to Loren. No, I cannot do tonight's talk justice, but finally my connection and love for music, literally my craving for music, makes perfect sense to me now.

*****

Today I felt, for lack of a better word, compelled to purchase pink roses "from Loren" to me. I have no doubt that they were indeed "from him" as a message that he and God are at work in my life. “There is no randomness” ...

Tonight I received a phone call which I pray is the beginning of reconciliation. I go to sleep with a hopeful heart and a certain peace I have not felt in some time.

*****

It is almost a year since you have been gone and for the first time tonight I tried sleeping on your side of the bed. A metaphor for my life ... it felt foreign and empty ... I am trying so hard to remember that I am NEVER ALONE ...

*****

The last few days have been filled with, as I refer to it, PTSD and tears remembering what was at this time last year. As I walked into my room a short while ago and looked up at this and I am reminded of how blessed I am.

Through all the pain I am so happy to know that I am still able to see the blessings in my life. I will never grow tired of the gorgeous sunsets, the beauty of the morning light or gazing at the stars and the moon in the night outside this window. I am healing ... and I am remembering that I am NEVER ALONE ...

*****

So much of this past year has been spent, as the saying goes, "going through the motions." Or possibly, just trying to survive.

Yes I know that loss is loss. Whether you are living with the death of a child, a sibling, a parent, a grandparent, a friend or your spouse, loss is loss. I also know that you cannot "rank" them as far as "what could be worse." But somehow I can't help but feel how very different each of these losses must be ... or maybe how it affects your life.

I cannot speak about the loss of a child, at least not in the physical sense, but I certainly can about the loss of a spouse. When you experience the death of your spouse, especially one that you spent more than half of your life with, in many ways you experience the death of part of yourself. I never used the words "he completes me", I don't happen to believe that anyone can "complete" us. If that were true the extraordinary love that Loren showed me all the years we were married I would never have felt that I lacked anything about who I was. That was and IS for me to figure out. But he was most definitely a PART of me. We grew up together, every decision made was made together. When I was struggling and in pain, he was as well. We were rarely apart throughout our marriage and to say that I have felt lost and alone in all aspects of my life would be an understatement.

Even going to church is a challenge. Church was a place where we were always together, side by side, and now to sit there alone, yes, even with all of the people surrounding me, I feel alone. Participating in the liturgy is almost impossible, because being there I am constantly reminded of Loren and his deep faith and I spend much of the time reliving much of our last year together, because "faith" was an enormous part of that time.

This morning was no different, but more difficult, as has been the past week. My thoughts are constantly going back to this time last year. As I sat in mass this morning I could not concentrate on what was going on. I kept asking God, "What do you have planned for me? What is it you want me to do? What journey do you want me to take without Loren by my side?" I have struggled with this every day since Loren went HOME, but even more so recently. I even told one of my friends this week that I have felt "useless."

Praying for a change of mind and heart ...

*****

A year ago, on Good, Friday each moment that went by it was becoming more apparent that Loren was preparing heart, mind and body to "go Home."

I spent the day trying to convince the charge nurse at the hospice to allow Loren to attend Easter Vigil in the chapel the next evening. Over and over she would say, "I'm not sure if that will be possible." I was not going to give up. You see, the year before he was so ill and missed all of the Holy Week services, and Holy Saturday we ended up in the ER where we received the news that would change our lives...forever. Most certainly mine.

Easter Sunday we were in intensive care in the hospital in Atlanta. Throughout the entire year of his illness he would speak often about how he had not been able to attend Holy Week or Easter services. Finally on Saturday I literally backed the charge nurse into a corner and told her in no uncertain terms that Loren would be in the chapel for Easter Vigil.

I will never ever forget that experience nor will the chaplain at that time. Loren's bed was rolled in and placed right next to the statue of The Blessed Mother who he was so devoted to. He was agitated from the move and was in pain. I looked up at Her and told Loren to do the same. I whispered to him to pray with me, and we recited the Hail Mary over and over again until the mass began. I held his hand throughout the service, just as we always did when we attended mass, and at one point I looked down at him. He had a tear rolling down his face and as the chaplain began blessing the water we both looked at him. He had the most beautiful smile on his face. He told me afterwards that he had never witnessed anything so beautiful, and it would stay with him always. I fought with and for Loren for an entire year. Many battles my hands were tied, but this one was one I was ecstatic to have won.

I will remember that night forever. I know The Blessed Mother was holding his other hand and whispering to him, "I am with you now and I will be with you at the hour of your death my faithful one."

*****

I stopped to have my hair cut on the way home from work today. The stylist shared with me that her father has recently died, and she shared about the pain she has been experiencing physically and emotionally. She also shared how she has "tried not to cry in front of her kids". Then she said, "I don't know how you have done this." Where to start? First, it is important to realize that "doing this" is a lifelong journey. We will not wake up one morning and say, "I am healed." We will heal forever after the death of someone we love, but we can, if we allow ourselves to be happy and LIVE our life knowing that our loved ones are cheering us on. After all, aren't they having THE most spectacular life now? Why should I be miserable? I will be the first one to admit that I can have difficult days (there have been many recently). But I get moving and kick butt each day as I close the door behind me and get out there among the world.

But this is what I have learned ... we've GOT to build a world where we ALLOW each other to mourn! Why can't we cry when someone we love has died? Why are we uncomfortable with each other's pain? Why do we have to be a martyr and have a stiff upper lip because my pain is too uncomfortable for someone else to see? Why should we feel weak if we DO that in front of someone else? By not mourning, by not sharing our pain we continue to cause ourselves even greater pain.

Please don't tell someone they need to "move on because it has been such and such amount of time." Instead be their safe place to fall. Let them know you are there for them to "share their story" for as much and as long as they need. The reality is that it could be years before someone is ready "to do" the work that it takes to even BEGIN healing.

One thing is for certain, death will touch each and every one of us. We have to begin to understand that to "learn to live again" will take time, patience and understanding ... from ALL of us. It will be YOUR turn to mourn if you are not already. Think about the love and understanding you will want around you ... then BE that for someone else NOW.

I do find solace knowing that others are on this same journey ... they HAVE, and I AM learning to live again ...

~

April 2016

~

*****

It is April and it is days away from the one-year anniversary of Loren's death. Tonight I am spending time with my two little grandsons. During dinner, our oldest grandson looks up at my son, his daddy and completely out of the blue says, "Papa is in my heart daddy" ... be still my heart ...

*****

Grief ... many things have caused me pain in this past year ... being out and about and seeing couples walking hand in hand, laughing at things you know only they understand. A glance between them that speaks so many unspoken words. I sit and wonder as I look at them, "what are they discussing, what are they planning together" and I wonder if they know, like I do now, how their life as they know it can change in just a beat of their hearts? I find myself so often wanting to walk up to them and ask them if they know how blessed they are to have the gift of that moment.

Easter Sunday mass ... nearly unbearable, but I sat there. Overcome throughout the service with memories of last year and how I am so close to being an entire year since Loren died. One year. One year without his embrace that he gave me each day. I never realized how much I took that for granted, something seemingly so simple, but when you don't have it you realize just how important and yes, even life giving it is. God how I miss it. I miss so much. I could literally fill the pages of a book with just the things I have missed since he has been gone.

Today was yet one more thing that causes me such pain ..."nothing makes me happier ... and nothing makes me sadder"...

One whole year ... and Logan keeps his Papa "in his heart." To hear him talk about Loren makes my heart both sing and break. So bittersweet. I wonder when the pain will no longer be there? Or will it always be there? Grief ... I'm trying so hard to make a life. One without so much pain ... I'm trying so hard. It's a lot of work. Realizing that an entire year has almost passed makes me realize that life isn't going to stop and wait for me ... I just have to continue moving forward and believe that I am NEVER ALONE.

*****

The decision to leave the place that Loren and I built together and raised our family was not necessarily a difficult one. Somehow I intuitively knew that to stay there would be far too painful for so many reasons.

Even after making the decision there were nights as the process began that I would lay awake crying but then there was "the voice". A voice I know is not mine. The voice would tell me that I was in fact making the right decision. That HE "will be with me". That God ... and indeed Loren ... would be with me.

At times in the year since Loren's death the voice has been relentless. Sometimes it has been difficult for me to trust. At the times I have, I have been filled with unbelievable peace. So it was with the decision to find a new home. And I have often said that I had felt "led" to my new home ... by Loren.

I enjoy decorating. The "concept" when I first purchased my new home was completely different from what it ended up becoming. As the days, weeks and months progressed I found myself drawn to nests. A new "theme", if you will, began to emerge as I began to dig deep, to do "the work" and to begin healing in my new home. My own "sanctuary" began to emerge. Something I was not even aware was happening. Having seen a presentation using the center photo and my own photos of the nests I had collected for my new home I realized I had indeed created my "sanctuary".

It is absolutely my "safe" place to be. A place that I long to be when I am not here. A place where when the moment I step through the door I exhale. I am at peace here and although physically Loren was never here, I feel his presence continually. I am surrounded by his calm, peaceful presence that he exuded in life. How blessed am I? Very. I am coming to the realization that it is possible to feel safe once again ... it is work to do so. Every day. But this "place" helps me ... and I created it ...

I am NEVER ALONE.

Center Photo by Permission

*****

"Let us run with perseverance
the race marked out for us".
Hebrews 12:1

I have spent a lot of the past few days "running." Running away from memories that at times are way too painful to sit with. Today while spending time "running" I went into a little shop where I had not been for a while but the lady behind the counter remembered me. We had a lovely conversation, and the anniversary of Loren's death tomorrow came up. She had some beautiful and comforting things to say to me and I looked at her and said, as I have many, many times throughout this past year, "As difficult as this has been Loren was obedient in the journey that was put in front of him, and I intend to be obedient to the one that has been put in front of me." No sooner had I said it I looked up and saw this verse. I have seen it before, many times. But today I felt as if it had been put right there just for me. A reminder. As tomorrow is on the horizon I continue to tell myself to hold on ... and to do my best to remember that I am NEVER ALONE.

*****

Just in case. Just in case you wonder. This is what grief "feels" like. This is what grief "looks" like. Some days. Some days even after "all this time"... this is what "it" looks and feels like ... still.

I had a conversation in the work place this week about just this. I told the person I was talking with, "I'm going to be the teacher today." I told him that there are a lot of broken people walking around in this world because the world wants us to be "all better." Three months, six months, nine months, a year after the death of someone we love. But we aren't. We aren't because the world does not want to "see" our pain. The world does not want to "feel" our pain. They want us to walk down the hallways of our workplaces and when asked, "How are you"? they want us to put a smile on our faces and say, "I'm good" or "I'm doing okay" and they walk away taking a deep breath ..."Phew good, she's doing 'good'"...The truth is, that because everyone wants you to "be okay" you haven't been able to share "your story" enough. The truth is that until you are able to tell your story enough, it will take you longer to begin healing. So you continue to get up and walk through the world in grief.

One year out, most days, you feel like you've "got this". You have figured out what your life is going to be like and maybe you have made peace with it ... maybe. Then life happens. You experience things that are painful, and it brings you right back to "the beginning". Or so you think.

Hopefully if you are living with the death of someone you love these days are few and far between. I have come to a place where I allow myself to feel like this. I don't beat myself up. I "go with the flow". Because some days the physical pain of grief brings you right back to the start. But I don't stay there long ... I don't want to. There is life out there to live and Loren most certainly wants me to live it. "I just want you to be okay."

I am honey ... I'm doing my best ... I am ... and I am doing my best to remember that I am NEVER ALONE ...

*****

Today was quite an emotional rollercoaster. We started the day at school with a beautiful chorus concert by our students and it began with a tribute to our music teacher who had died earlier in the school year.

She was a force of nature and I know without a doubt she was filling that room with her presence. I know our hearts were full of memories of her. And mine with Loren.

The children sang popular songs from Broadway shows and as they began to sing the most well-known song from the Broadway show Rent, "Seasons of Love", I struggled to hold it together.

This song became an anthem of sorts for me throughout Loren's illness. Loren did not make it a full 525,600 minutes in his journey. Just yesterday I wrote a friend and shared that as difficult a road it was, I had to try each day to remember what a miracle it was to wake up to and to go to sleep next to Loren each day during that time. I realized how important it was to measure our lives in the "day lights and the sunsets, the cups of coffee, and the laughter" because we may not be given 525,600 minutes ... we may not have all the "seasons of love" that we might want with those we love. In other words, cherish each moment of each day we are given. Loren and I were in a new season of love in our lives when life's most unimaginable happened.

Then the children began to sing the song "For Good" from Wicked. I have always believed that each of us comes into one another's lives for a purpose. The length of time does not matter. It could even be a moment. "Because I knew you I have been changed for good."

Sacred tears as I sat and listened to both of these songs today. I was reminded of how my life has been both changed and blessed by "Lovely Loren" as one of my friends has referred to him, in my life, and by walking with him through his illness and most certainly by his death.

At the end of the workday, we gathered together in our final meeting of the year and we said goodbye to staff members leaving and retiring. Always a difficult time, but another reminder of how we can have such an incredible impact on each other's lives. "525,600 minutes, 525,000 journeys to plan, 525,600 minutes, how do you measure the life of a woman or a man?" Maybe it's as simple as being present with and for one another in the times we are needed most.

Maybe it's as simple as that.

*****

Today, one year ago you returned HOME.

To you my love,

Loren…

How is it possible that an entire year has passed

Since the day you died?

How is it possible that I have even continued to live

Since that day?

So many days throughout that last year together I wondered how I could possibly go on in this life without you. WOULD I be able to?

You told me from the first day of learning what was happening

In our lives, and nearly every day afterward "I just want you to be okay."

Did you know what you were asking me to do?

Did you believe that I could?

Did you truly believe that I could be "okay" without you by my side?

You always did believe in me far more than I believed in myself.

One year ago, I sat next to you, watching you, knowing that you were

Leaving your physical body with every breath you were taking.

Wanting to ask you to stay, but whispering instead for you to…"Go to HIM."

I will never forget those last moments. Those moments when I wrapped my arms

Around you holding my hands to your chest as a tear rolled down your face

You opened your eyes, closed them, sighed your last breath in this world,

And breathed your first in the presence of God.

As difficult as it is to say,

Through the journey of your illness and your death

I have become someone I didn't know I could be.

Someone who is strong, someone who is courageous.

Did you know that you were asking me to be these things?

Did you know who I could become?

I hope I am making you proud.

Since the day we said "I do" we were one. And although we had our difficult moments

A life without you was unfathomable to me.

We were only children when we married.

We grew up together and our plan, our hope, our wish

Was to grow old together. That was not given to us.

I walked beside you every day in what would be

Our last year together, and yet now, at times I feel I am living someone else's life.

I have had to learn to live my life without you beside me.

Only recently have I realized that you do walk beside me, every hour of every day.

I cannot see you, but when I am still I can feel you.

The many details of life that have
Filled most of my days since you returned to HIS presence had
Kept me from feeling you near.
As life has quieted and there has been more time
To sit in the calm and in the silence, I can feel you.
You speak to me in the stillness of the dark nights and
As I look out across the stars in the sky you tell me,
"I am here."
Like I did for you as you went HOME to our Father,
You wrap your arms around me and hold my hands as
I clasp your cross to my heart. You comfort me and
You listen as I speak words of thanks to HIM who has
Walked with me each day during this past year since you walked Into HIS loving embrace.
"Live Every Moment, Laugh Every Day,
Love Beyond Words"
Such quiet, unassuming words that say so much.
We tried our best to do all of these things
Throughout our life together, not in grand ways but
In loving and simple ways,
Especially as we journeyed that last year beside one another.
Each day since you have been gone I have asked myself
Will I ever feel that I am "living every moment",
Or just existing in this world?
Will I ever be able to "laugh every day"
And truly feel joy again?
Can I even imagine "love beyond words"
with Anyone but you?

Life without you has not been easy.
I miss you as much today as I did the day I
Had to say goodbye to you.
Each day has been a choice.
A choice to "be okay."
A choice to put my feet on the floor and to
Walk out the door and live,
A choice to continue to say "Yes"
To a life that holds so many unknowns for me
and to live it Without you by my side.
I want to do all of this for you,
Because you wanted me to.
Thank you my love.
Thank you for giving all of yourself
to me and to your family.
Thank you for spending your whole life loving me
and taking care of me,
And continuing to do so, even now.
Thank you for loving me so much that you fought every day
To stay with me as long as you could.
Thank you for showing me that I was worthy of such a beautiful love.
Thank you for spending the rest of your life with me.
You will always be part of my heart and my soul.
I will love you and carry you with me ... Always.
I Am Never Alone.

*****

One year ago today family and friends gathered to celebrate Loren's life.

I have spent time this morning, as I do most mornings since his death, reflecting on who Loren was in my life and the things that I so loved about him. This morning for some reason I am remembering some of the physical "things" I loved most about him, because let's be real, it is the physical things we tend to be drawn to at first as we begin to develop a relationship with someone. You know, that feeling of WHOA when first meeting.

For me it was eight months before I actually met Loren in person. My brother was home for Christmas and was sharing pictures of his friends from the Air Force. When I first saw a picture of Loren and asked who he was and when he was going to bring him home with him I was told, " when you get your head on straight." Ummm, whatever brother.

Eight months later in August of 1978 Loren came home with my brother who was getting married. Do you believe in love at first sight? I do. Because it happened to me. Totally, ridiculously head over heels. Everyone around us knew it. I knew by the time he left a few days later I would spend my life with him. I recall my mom saying sometime shortly after that one day, "You're going to marry him."

This morning I am remembering one of his physical attributes I was most attracted to. And it's probably not something most women are first attracted to. His hands. I have always loved hands. Hands and eyes. Both features that say so much about a person. Eyes can "speak" so much emotion, but hands can as well. The gentleness of which someone uses them can say so much about a person. Loren's hands were beautiful. Physically beautiful. There was an elegance about his hands that normally you don't see in a man's hands. Long and elegant fingers but there was also a strength there, and I loved nothing more than when he reached over and took my hand in his and just held it. I spent a lot of time in the year of his illness just holding his hands. Stroking them and remembering how very much I loved them.

Today take the time to stop and remember those things you loved and still love about your beloved. Remember the things that made you realize you were falling in love with him or her. I wonder if they even know what that was? I would tell Loren from time to time how much I loved his hands. I'm not sure if he knew really how much I did and what they said to me about who he was. Take the time to SAY those things that lay in your heart. We never know if we will have the chance to share those things ... if not now, when?

*****

I read a quote on the internet the other day that went something like this: "Grief has a way of making time fly by while making life stand still." It is exactly how I have been describing this journey of grief to anyone who chooses to take the time to listen. Which in all honesty is very few people, as I was to learn in the beginning of this journey. I get it. It's painful. Especially to those who were close to you...

As I complete this book I have now journeyed through grief for six years. "Time flies by while life stands still." And every year at this time I am aware of the time I spend living both in the present and in the past.

This particular time of the year as I draw closer to the date of Loren's passing is a very tender time for me ... always, I don't choose it to be. It just is. So many memories come flooding back to me ... what was happening to Loren ... where we were ... those "words"... “there is nothing more that we can do” ... the ones that we had hoped and prayed we would never hear. And with all of that I move between that time ... the present time ... and all the way back ... to the beginning. Remembering when I first "met" Loren.

Yes, this time is most tender. I want it not to be. It just is. And so I have given myself permission to feel all that I need to feel, to mourn all that I need to mourn ... what was, what is not, what never will be in my life with Loren. Grief ... it certainly can make "life stand still"... and in these past six years of my life, try as I might, my heart and my soul has not received what I have longed to have in my life once again. Peace. So I continue to be gentle with myself. I continue to give myself permission to move from one place to the other ... from the present to the past.

I know so many who mourn the loss of a loved one, be it their spouse, a child, a parent, a friend. Remember that grief never ends ... it changes over time ... be the person who looks at someone who grieves the loss of a loved one and says, "come hold my hand, come lay your head on my shoulder," invite them to mourn in the safety of your love for them ... they not only want you to, but they need you to.

And always lift them up in prayer as they continue their walk ... and help them to know that they are ...

NEVER ALONE.

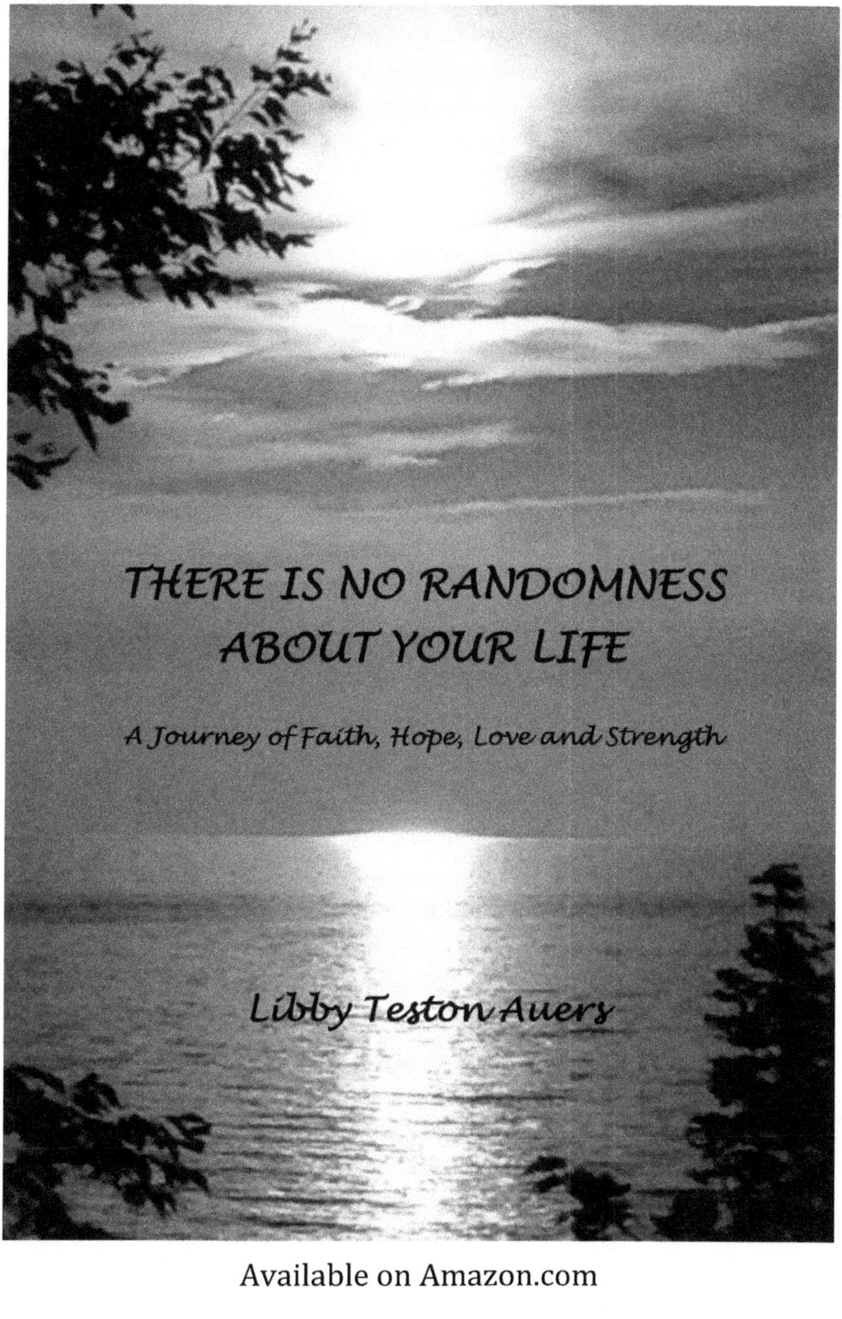
THERE IS NO RANDOMNESS
ABOUT YOUR LIFE
A Journey of Faith, Hope, Love and Strength
Libby Teston Auers

www.ingramcontent.com/pod-product-compliance
Lightning Source LLC
Chambersburg PA
CBHW060237050426
42448CB00009B/1474
9781736222249